Life During the **French** **Revolution**

by Gail B. Stewart

Lucent Books, P.O. Box 289011, San Diego, CA 92198-9011

Titles in The Way People Live series include:
    Cowboys in the Old West
    Life During the French Revolution
    Life in an Eskimo Village
    Life in the Warsaw Ghetto

Library of Congress Cataloging-in-Publication Data

Stewart, Gail, 1949–
    Life during the French Revolution / by Gail B. Stewart.
        p.   cm. — (Way people live)
    Includes bibliographical references and index.
    ISBN 1-56006-078-6
    1. France—Social life and customs—18th century—Juvenile
literature.   2. France—History—Revolution, 1789–1799—Social
aspects—Juvenile literature.   3. Social classes—France—
History—18th century—Juvenile literature.   I. Title.
II. Series.
    DC159.S74   1995
    944.04—dc20   94-40078
                                                                            CIP

Contents

Discovering the Humanity in Us All

The Way People Live series focuses on pockets of human culture. Some of these are current cultures, like the Eskimos of the Arctic; others no longer exist, such as the Jewish ghetto in Warsaw during World War II. What many of these cultural pockets share, however, is the fact that they have been viewed before, but not completely understood.

To really understand any culture, it is necessary to strip the mind of the common notions we hold about groups of people. These stereotypes are the archenemies of learning. It does not even matter whether the stereotypes are positive or negative; they are confining and tight. Removing them is a challenge that's not easily met, as anyone who has ever tried it will admit. Ideas that do not fit into the templates we create are unwelcome visitors—ones we would prefer remain quietly in a corner or forgotten room.

The cowboy of the Old West is a good example of such confining roles. The cowboy was courageous, yet soft-spoken. His time (it is always a he, in our template) was spent alternatively saving a rancher's daughter from certain death on a runaway stagecoach, or shooting it out with rustlers. At times, of course, he was likely to get a little crazy in town after a trail drive, but for the most part, he was the epitome of inner strength. It is disconcerting to find out that the cowboy is human, even a bit childish. Can it really be true that cowboys would line up to help the cook on the trail drive grind coffee, just hoping he would give them a little stick of pep-

permint candy that came with the coffee shipment? The idea of tough cowboys vying with one another to help "Coosie" (as they called their cooks) for a bit of candy seems silly and out of place.

So is the vision of Eskimos playing video games and watching MTV, living in prefab housing in the Arctic. It just does not fit with what "Eskimo" means. We are far more comfortable with snow igloos and whale blubber, harpoons and kayaks.

Although the cultures dealt with in Lucent's The Way People Live series are often historically and socially well known, the emphasis is on the personal aspects of life. Groups of people, while unquestionably affected by their politics and their governmental structures, are more than those institutions. How do people in a particular time and place educate their children? What do they eat? And how do they build their houses? What kinds of work do they do? What kinds of games do they enjoy? The answers to these questions bring these cultures to life. People's lives are revealed in the particulars and only by knowing the particulars can we understand these cultures' will to survive and their moments of weakness and greatness.

This is not to say that understanding politics does not help to understand a culture. There is no question that the Warsaw ghetto, for example, was a culture that was brought about by the politics and social ideas of Adolf Hitler and the Third Reich. But the Jews who were crowded together in the ghetto cannot be understood by the Reich's politics. Their life was a day-to-day battle for existence, and the creativity and methods they used to prolong their lives is a vital story of human perseverance that would be denied by focusing only on the institutions of Hitler's Germany. Knowing that children as young as five or six outwitted Nazi guards on a daily basis, that Jewish policemen helped the Germans control the ghetto, that children attended secret schools in the ghetto and even earned diplomas—these are the things that reveal the fabric of life, that can inspire, intrigue, and amaze.

Books in the The Way People Live series allow both the casual reader and the student to see humans as victims, heroes, and onlookers. And although humans act in ways that can fill us with feelings of sorrow and revulsion, it is important to remember that "hero," "predator," and "victim" are dangerous terms. Heaping undue pity or praise on people reduces them to objects, and strips them of their humanity.

Seeing the Jews of Warsaw only as victims is to deny their humanity. Seeing them only as they appear in surviving photos, staring at the camera with infinite sadness, is limiting, both to them and to those who want to understand them. To an object of pity, the only appropriate response becomes "Those poor creatures!" and that reduces both the quality of their struggle and the depth of their despair. No one is served by such two-dimensional views of people and their cultures.

With this in mind, the The Way People Live series strives to flesh out the traditional, two-dimensional views of people in various cultures and historical circumstances. Using a wide variety of primary quotations—the words not only of the politicians and government leaders, but of the real people whose lives are being examined—each book in the series attempts to show an honest and complete picture of a culture removed from our own by time or space.

By examining cultures in this way, the reader will notice not only the glaring differences from his or her own culture, but also will be struck by the similarities. For indeed, people share common needs—warmth, good company, stability, and affirmation from others. Ultimately, seeing how people really live, or have lived can only enrich our understanding of ourselves.

What Could Have Happened?

The new king was fat, especially in his face and neck. Not even the elaborate silk clothing he wore for the coronation ceremony could hide that. Nevertheless he had an air of strength and grandeur about him. His wig was powdered and curled, his shoes gleamed, and the white fur adorning his robes was luxurious. At his side stood his wife, nineteen-year-old Marie Antoinette. She was breathtaking in her flowing gown; the spangles and jewels were too numerous to count, and ostrich feathers adorned her shoulders.

She was, observers agreed, the more appealing half of the royal couple. And, aware of the scrutiny, she enjoyed every minute of it. "She walked beautifully," writes one historian, "apparently floating over the slippery parquet floors. . . . As for her dancing . . . when she failed to follow the music's beat, then the music was wrong."[1]

"Men Broke Down and Wept"

The date was June 11, 1775. The occasion was the coronation of the new French king, Louis XVI. His predecessor had died a year earlier, but France had observed a suitable period of mourning before the happy ritual of crowning the next king.

There had been murmurings about the high cost of the ceremony, the number of elegant balls and state dinners. In troubled

Louis XVI became king of France in 1775. Although the French had doubts about maintaining the opulence and expense of their ruler's lifestyle, tradition dictated it.

"Dare to Know!"

In the Time-Life volume entitled Winds of Revolution: Time Frame 1700–1800, *the editors reflect on the mood of the eighteenth century. In light of the revolutions under way in science and philosophy, it is not surprising that thinkers of the day questioned age-old political traditions as well.*

"From one end of Europe to the other, the anthem of the eighteenth century was the simple but dangerous word 'Why?' Time-honored certainties crumbled: Old assumptions about the authority of kings, the structure of the universe, even the very existence of God, were called into question. The thinkers of the age would take nothing on trust; old habits of unquestioning obedience to religious, political, and social authority were replaced by the scrutiny of all ideas under the penetrating light of human reason. Philosophers were exhilarated by the notion that theirs was a time of profound and accelerated change. Few would argue with their German contemporaries, who named the era *Die Aufklarung*—the Enlightenment.

'Dare to know!' commanded the German philosopher Immanuel Kant, expressing the spirit of the century. 'Have the courage to use your intelligence.'

In Britain, France, Italy, Switzerland, the Netherlands, and the German states, in Poland, Russia, and even in the far-off American colonies, writers and scholars rose to the challenge. But this intellectual ferment was not restricted to men of letters, scribbling away in their ivory towers. New ways of looking at the world would lead inexorably to bold attempts to change it: By the end of the century, an American republic would be born out of the throes of revolution; and in France, crowned heads would roll, and a monarchy would topple."

economic times, some wondered, wouldn't it be smarter to do without the splendor? Besides, others said, a French king ruled by divine right—by the grace of God. Certainly in God's eyes Louis XVI was already king, and no ceremony was necessary to make it official.

But there was really no way to stop it, even if most of the French people had wanted to—which they hadn't. Tradition and ceremony were intrinsic to royal transition. The new king would be anointed with special oils and allowed to carry the ceremonial staff of the great eighth-century king of the Franks, Charlemagne. He would pledge to uphold the peace of the church, to prevent disorder in his kingdom, and to impose justice. No one doubted the king's ability to govern, for again, he would do so with God's grace.

No matter how logical the arguments for doing without a coronation, the actual event inspired strong patriotic feeling in everyone. One historian reports that on that brilliant morning, after the ceremony, which took several hours in the cathedral at Rheims, "when . . . the cathedral doors were flung open to reveal the young monarch crowned and enthroned in glory, invested with the sceptre of Charlemagne and anointed with the holy oil of Clovis, men broke down and wept despite themselves."[2]

After the coronation, the new French king prepared to perform miracles, as was the custom for many centuries. According to the belief of the time, a touch from a newly anointed French king could cure scrofula, one of the most dreaded diseases of the day. More than twenty-four hundred coughing victims of the disease, with distorted features and foul-smelling skin, approached King Louis XVI and received the touch for which they had been waiting. There were, it seemed, no bounds to the new king's power.

"The Easiest People to Govern"

Throughout Europe the coronation of Louis XVI was viewed with interest, and some envy. The French were so organized, so structured. They did everything with such style and elegance. They set the standards for fashion, music, and architecture. Their government was both stable and lavish. "Their court was the most brilliant in Europe," writes one historian, "their aristocracy the most sophisticated; as for their politeness, it was legendary."[3]

The French Revolution brought more than bloodshed to France, but most people think first of the thousands of prisoners brought to their death by the guillotine.

Little wonder that their king had such an easy time of it:

The French, as everyone knew, were the easiest people to govern. . . . The French loved their monarch; even when, on occasion, they no longer did, they still obeyed his orders. The King of France, in fact, was much envied by his brethren: he ruled over a large, polished, disciplined nation; with the smallest of efforts, he could make himself extremely popular; the resources available to him were immense.[4]

How astonishing, then, that in less than eighteen years Louis XVI would be put to death, beheaded by his subjects—these, the "easiest people to govern." His government would topple, and the eight-hundred-year tradition of the French monarchy would come to a violent end.

Questions

This violent, turbulent period in French history, known as the French Revolution, began in 1789 and continued for nearly ten years. Unlike the American Revolution, which ended with a colony's independence from its mother country, the French Revolution was fought between Frenchmen and ended with no resolution of the unrest among the people. The decade was filled with social and political chaos, terror, and violence and bloodshed on an unparalleled scale—most of that via the guillotine.

The French Revolution *did* usher in, albeit in a very strong and clumsy way, the idea of the sovereignty of the people of a nation, regardless of their class or economic status. This was something new in Europe. And the Revolution

Crowds gather to watch an execution. The guillotine became the preferred method of executing political prisoners, gaining the name "the national razor."

gave birth to a host of political words still used today: the use of "left" and "right" to describe one's politics, and terms such as "anarchist," "bureaucrat," and "terrorist."

But it must be remembered that the French Revolution was a very human struggle. People lived and died during those years,

"The National Razor"

Nothing symbolizes the French Revolution as dramatically as the guillotine. Jokingly referred to as "the national razor," it was a large, heavy blade that could be raised and dropped between two posts connected at the top by a crossbar. When allowed to drop, the blade fell with such force that it severed the head of anyone lying on the platform beneath it. It was the most common method of executing enemies and suspected counterrevolutionaries during the French Revolution.

The guillotine was named after the man who advocated its use, Dr. Joseph-Ignace Guillotin. Although Dr. Guillotin did not invent the machine, he was the primary force behind the passage of a law in France that all death sentences would be carried out by its means. It was his belief that the guillotine was the most painless, most humane method of killing a human being.

Indeed, if one looks at the ways criminals were usually executed in those days, "painlessness" does not seem to have been a consideration. Writes historian Susan Banfield in *The Rights of Man, the Reign of Terror:* "An ordinance of 1670 included the following: hanging, having one's hands cut off or tongue cut out and then being hanged, being broken on a wheel, being strangled and then broken, being burned, being drawn apart by four horses, and having one's head cut off." The latter, historians agree, was the means reserved for criminals of noble birth.

educated their children, and fed their families. Some were key figures in the political and social movement; others were avid spectators; and others tried to stay as far from the action and violence as possible.

What could it have been like to live during those days? How did this "large, polished, disciplined nation" of the 1770s transform itself into a state of terror and violence? And who were the people who sparked and encouraged that transformation, to the point that that symbol of grisly death, the guillotine, was the most frequently used piece of machinery in the land?

Of Title and Privilege

Although the Revolution began suddenly in 1789 with great violence, the causes of the uprising were ancient. As one historian writes, "Like a very hot kettle of soup, the French Revolution simmered and bubbled without boiling over, not for days, months, or years, but for centuries."[5]

No single event or group of people caused the trouble; rather, trouble was rooted simply in the nature of French society. The *ancien regíme* ("old regime"), as the political and social system before the Revolution was called, was structured in ways that dated back many centuries, to the medieval age in Europe.

Those Who Have, Those Who Have Not

At the time of the French Revolution, as in medieval days, land was the only source of wealth. There was no manufacturing, no industry that brought in money in any substantial amounts. The crops people grew and the animals they raised were the products of land, and those who owned the land were in control. As one historian writes, "The possessors of land were the masters of those who needed it to work and to live."[6]

The owners of land were the nobles, those who had titles and position because

This depiction of a cattle and sheep farm in eighteenth century France is a bit idealized—rather than plump, happy, and content, the average French farmer was desperately poor through overtaxation.

their fathers and grandfathers and great-grandfathers had had titles and position. France was an aristocratic society, one in which power was acquired by the luck of one's birth. Powerful though they were, the aristocrats of France were not a majority. They numbered about a half million of France's population of more than twenty-six million.

The classes of French society were called estates. The First Estate was composed of the men and women of the church, the Second Estate of titled nobles, and the 25.5 million common people made up the Third Estate. A sixteenth-century document explains the locked-in relationship of the three estates in France, an explanation as applicable to prerevolutionary France as to the time when it was first written:

> The head is the King. The arms are the nobility. The feet are the Third Estate. The arms must carry food to the mouth. . . . The clergy is the heart. . . . Each must be kept in his Estate. . . . The three Estates are members of one body, of one province which is mother to all of them.[7]

Unrivalled in Power

The clergy—the First Estate—comprised less than 1 percent of the population of France, but was unrivalled in terms of overall power. The church was the Catholic Church, a decree by King Henry IV in 1598 having ordered all of France's people to follow that religion. In France, the church owned one-tenth of all the land. In certain areas of northern France, whole villages sat upon church land, and so were indebted to the clergy for the land's use. Taxes collected for the use of such land amounted to more than 150 million *livre* per year. (A livre was the equivalent of approximately $4.50 in modern American currency.)

In addition to such a large tax burden, French citizens were also required to tithe; that is, to pay the equivalent of one-tenth of the value of their home, their crops, their

The traditional apparel of the members of the three estates. (From left to right), the Second Estate, the Third Estate, and the First Estate.

NE' POUR LA PEINE

The lower classes resented the callous attitude most nobles and merchants had toward members of the Third Estate. French peasants led difficult lives. Not only did they have to maintain their farms, they often had to work in the city as well to supplement their incomes.

flocks, and their possessions to the church each year. Although in many cases the amount fell short of one-tenth, it was a large burden on the common people, who were already paying many other taxes.

Besides having such enormous wealth at its disposal, the church controlled all schools in France and held an absolute right of censorship of all printed material. The church's records of births, burials, and marriages were the most esteemed official documents in the nation, the highest authority when inheritances and titles of nobility had to be validat-

ed. And because the king ruled by divine right, it was unlikely that the monarchy would move to diminish the church's power in France. "Without the Catholic sacraments," one French historian declares, "the king had no legal existence."[8]

The clergy was as much political as it was religious. The king of France appointed abbots of large monasteries and bishops, for example. Such appointments were chosen from the ranks of the nobles, so it was virtually impossible for a common priest (who did come from the ranks of the commoners) to ascend to high church office.

This meant that the leaders of the church in France were not chosen for their adherence to their religion and so were not always well schooled in the religious life. Many had little knowledge of the sacraments or church ritual; their days in the clergy were spent collecting taxes or tithes, or keeping records for the parishes. One noble was forced to accept a career in the clergy because an injury made him unfit for the military. According to historian William Doyle, he was "ordained a subdeacon at 21, canon of [the large cathedral] Rheims within weeks, an abbot within months, yet did not become a priest until four years later."[9]

Deep Resentment

The higher offices of the church contrasted sharply with the common parish priest, whom the peasants respected. Most parish priests had been commoners before entering the priesthood. They had the same background and values as the rural peasants. The same was true of most nuns, who worked hard tending children in hospitals and orphanages.

Parish priests' incomes were small. They depended on token fees received for presiding over funerals, baptisms, and marriages. They were, in fact, barely distinguishable from the people they served. "Country priests, dressed in their threadbare habits," historian Susan Banfield writes, "spent their days trudging rough country roads to tend to the problems of those in their charge." [10] Later, when the commoners would rise up against the nobility, these lowly members of the First Estate would support the commoners.

It was the high clergy whom the common people resented. Their salaries were enormous—the modern equivalent of a six-figure salary for an archbishop, and even his lowly assistant earned twenty thousand livre. And though they collected their salaries from the taxes and tithes of the poor, they themselves paid no taxes whatsoever.

The behavior of these wealthy clergy members was a source of irritation to the commoners as well. Graft and corruption were common, as Banfield writes:

> Bishops abandoned the people in their dioceses to accept invitations to live at court. There, many traded their clerical robes for the fashionable silks of the courtiers and gave themselves over to a life of worldly power and riches. Well-to-do young women might spend several years in elegant convents, only to emerge more eligible marriage prospects than ever—because of their "sacrifice." [11]

Privilege by Blood

The aristocracy comprised members of the Second Estate, those who could trace their noble family trees back for many centuries. Many nobles could show titles going back to the Middle Ages. The nobles, it was believed, were related to the warriors who helped conquer the land of France in ancient times. They were men "of the sword," those whose power, courage, and service to France was beyond doubt.

"They formed a separate order or estate in society," writes Doyle, "and all the rest of the king's subjects, from the most wretched beggar to [a] great colonial shipper dining off plates were . . . commoners." [12] Another authority explains the nobility's attitude about their role in society: "They were a distinct race, heroic and military, made for command and insistent upon the marks of respect assured by honorific distinctions. How could such men dream of being confounded with the rest of the nation?" [13]

Members of the Second Estate—the nobility— enjoyed many economic and societal privileges. It was the vast inequality between the estates—and the callous attitudes of the nobility—that led to the French Revolution.

An Unfair Lord

To be a noble before the Revolution almost always involved the ownership of some land. As one group of irritated peasants wrote, the lord of their land treated them very unfairly. This excerpt is from Richard Cobb's book Voices of the French Revolution.

"[The lord] does not allow the removal of vine-stakes if it does not suit him and charges for the staking that he does want. He does not let us raise wool-bearing animals or build sheep-pens in the country.

He makes us pay him the same as the tithe on all grain, so that out of six sheaves, we pay one, tithe included.

He lays claim to, he even forbids us to sell produce from the cultivated land to outsiders; in this way he gets it for almost nothing.

The community is very poor because it does not have the same rights and privileges as others, so that the lord holds us as slaves."

About thirty thousand noble families lived at the time of the French Revolution. Although their numbers were small, they owned approximately one-third of the land in France. As nobles, they were also guaranteed certain privileges and honors that the majority of French people were not. For instance, nobles could carry swords in public, while commoners could not. They could display a coat of arms. In church, a noble's family could sit on the right side of the altar—the desired side, for it was supposed to be the equivalent of sitting "on the right hand of God," where Jesus is believed to sit. Also, a noble could be buried within the special inner court of the church when he died, rather than in the common cemetery.

A Host of Economic Privileges

Because the nobility were related to knights and ancient warriors, they were sometimes referred to as nobles "of the blood." And because they had spilled their blood to benefit France, the reasoning went, they were not expected to further contribute money. Nobles were granted exclusive economic privileges, a fact that often infuriated the common people.

The taxes that were so much a burden for the Third Estate were not imposed on the nobles. Nobility did not have to pay the *taille*, or direct tax. In fact, not paying the taille was, says one historian, "the quintessential badge of nobility."[14] It is true that the nobility had some small financial obligations to the government, but these could be offset easily by the feudal dues that nobles collected from commoners who lived or worked on their land.

The nobility had political power as well. As mentioned earlier, the higher church offices went to nobles. The same was true of the French army; nobles held all positions above the rank of captain. Almost every one of the king's advisers and ministers was titled. In fact, the king could only be approached face-to-face if one was part of the Second Estate.

"Vain, Proud, Poor, and Slothful"

However, as privileged as they were, not all nobles were wealthy. More than half of France's nobility were of average or below-average means, and some were actually poor. Whether from bad luck, laziness, or poor management of their inherited wealth, many nobles had fallen onto hard times. They lived on whatever feudal dues they could squeeze out of peasants in their districts, and had very little to show for it.

In 1763 one visitor to the region of Boulogne noted with some disdain how the nobles there lived in poverty, while trying unsuccessfully to maintain a superior attitude.

[They are] vain, proud, poor, and slothful. . . . They allow their country houses to go to decay, and their gardens and fields to waste; and reside in dark holes in the Upper Town . . . without light, air, or convenience. There they starve within doors, that they may have the wherewithal to purchase fine clothes, and appear dressed once a day.

More Than Wealth

In her book The Rights of Man, the Reign of Terror, *Susan Banfield explains that belonging to the nobility in prerevolutionary France entailed more than simply having money.*

"A farmer in the Loire valley was accustomed to working his own land. Throughout the growing season he and his youngest son labored under the hot sun. He was frugal with his money, careful to make his modest yearly income stretch to meet the expenses of his family and their ramshackle farmhouse. Not far off, in Nantes, another landowner enjoyed a fortune of several million *livres*. His sons had the best tutors and dressed in fine silks. To which orders did these two men belong?

The first was a noble, a member of the Second Estate, and the second was a commoner, or member of the Third Estate. The point here is that wealth was not what made someone a member of the nobility. There were a number of impoverished nobles who were forced to help with their own farmwork and to count their pennies. On the whole, however, the French nobility were a very wealthy group. All together they numbered about four hundred thousand—about one and a half percent of the country's total population—yet owned one fifth of the nation's lands—twice as much as the Church. Many nobles lived in elegant chateaux [country estates] and manor houses. Others, who lived at court with the King and Queen, might spend over forty thousand *livres* a year on dinner parties alone. A significant number of the nobles who lived in the provinces, however, lived modestly, with little to distinguish them outwardly from their nonnoble neighbors."

Members of the nobility, even if they had fallen on hard times, would become social pariahs if they did any form of work. Their social class demanded idleness, or they would lose their titles.

They have no education, no taste for reading, no housewifery, nor indeed any earthly occupation, but that of dressing their hair, and adorning their bodies. They hate walking, and would never go abroad, if they were not stimulated by the vanity of being seen. . . . They pretend to be jealous of their rank, and will entertain no correspondence with merchants, whom they term plebeians.[15]

Why didn't such nobles do some sort of work, and earn enough money to live in the style they so desperately affected? The answer was that they were absolutely constrained from doing so. Nobles were supposed to be idle. Working or engaging in a trade would be social suicide; it would be admitting that their privileged status was not self-perpetuating, that to exist they had to live like commoners.

Nobles who did work knew that they would be forced to give up their titles, a consequence that would bring them shame and embarrassment. Few chose to endanger their noble lifestyles by doing something as common as work. "In any case," explains one historian, "they had their children to think of; nobility was a family affair, a distinction only truly worth having if it could be passed down the generations."[16]

Instant Nobility

Alongside the long and honored tradition of the nobles of the blood existed another type of nobility. Since the reign of Louis XIV, who

"The Correct Thing for a Man of Fashion"

In her book My Scrap-Book of the French Revolution, *Elizabeth Wormeley Latimer quotes a man who lived through the Revolution in Paris. With a good eye for detail, he explains what the well-dressed Parisian wore in the days before the beginning of the Revolution.*

"Bonnets are worn only by great ladies and by wealthy *bourgeoises*. They are commonly of straw, tall in the crown, and trimmed with silk, ribbon, and lace. Emerald green intermixed with very bright pink is extremely fashionable. It is proper for ladies in public to carry a fan in one hand and a little velvet mask in the other, which however, is rarely put on.

Men think it good taste to dress simply in the street, in dark cloth, after the English fashion; soot color is very fashionable. The hats are tall, tapering, and have a silver buckle in the middle of their ribbon. . . . White stockings it is not good taste to wear on the street; they should be white with blue stripes. Men carry muffs occasionally, as well as the ladies.

It is the correct thing for a man of fashion to carry two watches, and to hold in the hand a bamboo cane with a gold knob, or one of porcelain. Dandies carry the cane up to the shoulder, like a musket.

Besides soot-color, coats are made of apple-green cloth, bottle-green, dead-leaf, and beef-blood. This last . . . is quite the rage. It is worn with a white silk waistcoat, and small-clothes made of satin. . . . If boots are worn they must be of soft leather; yellow top-boots are the height of the fashion, but only the most advanced dandies can venture to wear them. The hair is commonly powdered, but some men of rank have given up powder and have their hair simply tied behind with a black ribbon."

---

ruled France from 1643 to 1715, some wealthy members of the Third Estate could purchase nobility. In fact, in the years between Louis XIV and Louis XVI, more than ten thousand of these "instant nobles" were created.

What could have prompted such a break from tradition? Simply put—money. By allowing wealthy members of the bourgeoisie (the professionals and merchants of the Third Estate) to buy titles, Louis XIV and the kings who succeeded him brought huge sums of money into the royal treasury, money that was desperately needed to keep the monarchy solvent.

Many of the new nobility purchased positions in France's judicial system as judges, court officers, and even bailiffs. Because of the high population of "instant nobles" in the courts, the newcomers were often referred to as nobles "of the robe," so called because of the robes worn in court.

During the first years of Louis XVI, more than fifty thousand offices were ennobling ones; that is, positions that would ensure title and honor. And the money those offices generated was still needed; historians estimate that nobles of the robe contributed more than a billion livres to the sagging French economy of the late eighteenth century.

A Source of Tension

But the presence of so many new nobles was a source of social tension and friction. For one thing, merchants and wealthy businessmen who had not achieved title were angry and jealous of those that had. As William Doyle comments, "Nothing enraged the professional bourgeoisie more than to see self-made businessmen leapfrogging them into the highest levels of society." [17]

Those who could not afford the steep price of a seat in the judicial system, or the fifty thousand livres needed to buy a regiment in the French army, had to stand back and watch as others who had the money acquired social status. They did have a few options, however. Many tried to marry into wealthy families, and such marriages of convenience became increasingly common in France. Others even paid forgers to counterfeit a noble genealogy—a minor industry during the eighteenth century.

Hostility toward these instant nobles was not limited to the jealous bourgeoisie. There were plenty of nobles of the blood who looked down their noses at the new nobility as nothing more than pretenders. The poor nobles, especially whom Doyle calls "the threadbare gentry with impeccable lineages but no resources," felt that their traditional position as honored, respected aristocrats was being threatened—and there was nothing they could do about it. [18]

By the late 1770s, in fact, irritated nobles had put so much pressure on the king that gradually certain positions were closed to members of the Third Estate, no matter how wealthy. Several courts banned from their ranks people who couldn't prove that their nobility went back five generations. In the army, too, high ranks were gradually closed to those whose nobility could not be verified for less than four generations. Little by little, the acquired privileges of the wealthy members of the Third Estate were being stripped away, and the bourgeoisie was furious.

CHAPTER 2

The Downtrodden

While wealthy members of the Third Estate were growing increasingly angry over the loss of opportunity to attain nobility, most of France's people were worried about feeding their families. For the majority of the common people—those who were not professionals or rich merchants—survival was the only goal.

Predators of All Kinds

More than 80 percent of the class known as the Third Estate were peasants, who lived on farms in the rural areas of France. Their lives were like something out of an old fairy tale, full of menace and magic.

Peasants were constantly threatened by wolves. Wolves lay in wait for children, shepherds, and unlucky travelers. People knew that they risked their lives when going out alone in a forest, for they could be torn to bits by the ferocious beasts.

If one avoided the wolves, criminals roaming the countryside in multitudes presented another danger. "Worst of all," writes one historian, "were the armed bands, often masked, banging at a farmhouse door, threatening to set fire to a house and barn, stealing, sometimes killing, a threat to country folk as well as to travelers, especially in borderlands, in highlands, and in forested regions."[19] Fear of strangers in the rural areas was not reactionary in eighteenth-century France—it was considered prudent.

A Violent Way of Life

Thus, life was surprisingly violent for the peasants of France in the late eighteenth century. Fights, robberies, and assassinations on the country roads were common occurrences. So, too, were episodes of family violence—knifings, beatings of wives and children, and even the deliberate killing of an infant, which occurred in families too large for parents to feed and clothe all their young.

Blood, suffering, and death were accepted parts of life. As social historian J.F. Bosher remarks, the deaths of little children from accident and disease "were so common that many parents did not bother to attend burial ceremonies."[20]

Government officials engaged in the business of death quite frequently, and quite publicly. Both in rural villages and in large cities, convicted criminals were flogged and tortured, and supposed witches were burned at the stake or stoned—all perfectly acceptable forms of punishment. In one execution, well attended by masses of commoners in 1757, a murderer was slowly tortured to death by the most painful method the courts could devise. Writes Bosher:

> Strapped down naked before a huge crowd, [the criminal] lay shrieking with his right hand fixed in a fire of burning sulfur (which set alight the straw under his head) while boiling liquid was poured into holes cut in his flesh (ten minutes).

Then his four limbs were attached to horses (twenty minutes), and he was slowly pulled to pieces; but he proved exceptionally strong so the hangmen had to loosen his joints with a knife (four minutes). [The criminal] watched his arms being pulled off and then died.[21]

Secret Rites and Magic Spells

Although peasants, by official dictate, were required to belong to the Catholic Church, as it was practiced it was heavily laden with ancient pagan custom. Peasants knew that to cure a fever, or an animal bite, or any number of other ailments and injuries, it was necessary to have a supply of secret magic words and incantations in addition to prayers and vigils. It was not, as some church officials worried, that the peasants had no faith in God or the saints. They did; but they believed that there were magical ways of gaining the attention of such powers.

For instance, various saints were linked with specific diseases. One prayed to Saint Sebastian for relief from the plague, Saint Lazare for eczema or rashes, Saint Hubert

"It Smelled Like a Stable"

In his book, Liberty! Equality! Fraternity!: The Story of the French Revolution, *Clifford Lindsey Alderman describes a typical home of a peasant family in 1789.*

"Jacques Deschenaux had once owned a house and farm, inherited from his father. A host of troubles—crop failures, an epidemic among his herd, his wheat leveled by a hailstorm and, above all, his crushing taxes—had forced him to sell his property.

The house in which the family lived was neither better nor worse than those of most other peasants in the village. It was low-built, of clay and straw cased in by wooden beams, and had a thatched roof. Inside there was only one room, and in it they all ate and slept.

It was not a comfortable place, this house which had been built a century earlier in the time of Louis XIV, nor was it very clean. Its overhead beams were blackened with the smoke of years, its floor was hard-trodden earth, and its walls, once whitewashed, were covered with brownish mold. It smelled like a stable, and with good reason. A door at the back of the room led to an attached cattle shed, while at the front a constant trickle of liquid seeped in from the manure pile, used for fertilizer, which by long custom among all peasants was always placed just outside the front door. But the family was used to such squalor and thought nothing of it, for there was no prospect that things would ever be better for them.

Inside the house on a summer day, the family [was sitting down] to their midday meal. Jacques and his two boys wore woolen jackets and breeches of a material called *fort-en-diable,* meaning 'strong as the devil.' *Mere* (Mother) Deschenaux and ten-year-old Clothilde had on simple dresses and aprons. All wore wooden sabots [sandals] on their feet. The mother was serving a watery cabbage soup."

for rabies, and Saint Apolline for an end to toothache pain. The methods of gaining the favor of the particular saint varied—sometimes candles lit, sometimes a long series of magic words repeated quickly several times, and sometimes even consultation with a soothsayer or sorcerer. As Doyle observes: "Christianity remained for many, on the eve of the Revolution, what it had been in the 17th century and before: one of the elements of a popular religion in which faith and superstition were inextricably mixed."[22]

Carrying the Weight of France on Their Backs

Members of the Third Estate were desperately poor. Visitors to France were appalled at the conditions among the peasants. Arthur Young, an English traveler whose detailed descriptions of the countryside are invaluable to historians, observed that "all the country girls and women are without shoes or stockings; and the plowmen at their work have neither sabots [wooden shoes] nor stockings to their feet. This is a poverty that strikes at the root of national prosperity. . . . It reminded me of the misery of Ireland."[23]

Poverty was everywhere, so pervasive in the Third Estate that it was impossible for the peasants to imagine life free from it. Most peasants doubted that the government cared. Many even doubted that high officials knew how wretched conditions were. "Sire King!" pleaded one letter from the peasants of Angoulime, "if only you knew what was happening in France and what great misery and poverty your humble people suffer!"[24]

Whether the king knew or cared mattered very little, for the economic woes of the common people were woven into the social and economic fabric of French life. As mem-

A cartoon from the period before the French Revolution illustrates a common theme, and a common complaint of the Third Estate—peasants felt as though they carried the financial weight of the clergy and nobility upon their backs.

bers of the lower class, the peasants and other commoners had an astonishing number of taxes and responsibilities, burdens that did not trouble the First or Second Estates. So heavy a load did the common people carry, in fact, that many popular cartoons were variations on a common theme: a farmer bent over, groaning, as two fat men—one a noble, the other a bishop—sit on his back, laughing.

Taxes, Tithes, and Other Responsibilities

In addition to the basic taille and tithe paid by the Third Estate, peasants paid a poll tax based on income, an excise tax on soap and playing cards, and a tax called "twentieth-tax," which claimed one-twentieth of a person's income. Peasants were more heavily penalized than others simply because an ancient social system called feudalism still existed in the countryside. During the Middle Ages, rulers granted lords large territories of land as rewards for loyalty or payments for military service. Since it was considered beneath a lord to farm land himself, he "allowed" poor peasants, then called serfs, to do the work for him. The lord would then charge the serfs rent and take the lion's share of the crops grown and the flocks raised. In return, the serfs would have a small dwelling and a little food to live on.

But in eighteenth-century France many nobles who were lords by title no longer owned the land that their ancestors had owned. They had sold their lands back to the king. Feudalism as an economic system had ended in the Middle Ages throughout most of Europe. Even so, because of blood ties with the old lords, many French nobles continued to exact the same dues and force the same responsibilities on peasants that their ancestors imposed. Arthur Young noted, "In passing through many of the French provinces, I was struck with the various and heavy complaints of the farmers and little proprietors of the feudal grievances with which their industry was burdened."[25]

Peasants were forbidden to sell any of their crops until after the nobles had sold their share at a higher price. Peasants were forced to pay fees for the privilege of using a lord's grain mill or winepress. Such fees were almost laughable—they were collected whether or not the lord even owned a mill or a winepress!

Another vestigial feudal responsibility was called the *corvée*. This law required peasants and their families to leave home each year for between six and thirty days at a time to work on the roads. The peasants were not only expected to provide uncompensated labor, but also were supposed to bring wagons and teams of animals to pull those wagons. The corvée took millions of people away from their fields each year, and their crops and flocks suffered for it.

Age-old laws that gave lords exclusive hunting privileges on the land were also troublesome to the peasants. The peasants were prohibited from killing or chasing off animals such as deer and wild boar, which destroyed their crops. Nobles were afraid that if the peasants disturbed the nesting places or the hiding spots of the game they would ruin the hunting. So peasants in eighteenth-century France fumed as they watched nobles ride carelessly through their vegetable gardens and wheat fields, trampling the crops in pursuit of wild animals.

An Agrarian Crisis

One factor contributing to the poverty among the peasants was inefficient farming practices. In fact, for years leading up to the French Revolution, harvests were smaller than normal. French agriculture suffered from inept land management, wasteful practices, and woefully outdated technology.

Not that the land itself was poor. Quite the contrary: France had some of the most fertile land in Europe. The soil was rich and the climate perfect for many crops. However, the nobles who owned large amounts of the land did not live on the land; rather, they rented it to peasants, who knew nothing of modern agriculture. "The fields are scenes of pitiable mismanagement," wrote Arthur Young, "yet all this country highly improvable if they knew what to do with it . . . the property, perhaps, of some of those glittering beings who figured in the procession the other day at [the king's palace]."[26]

Even those few peasants who owned their own land were unwilling to try new methods. Their plots of land were small and narrow, and they grew barely enough to feed their families. Besides, a large portion of the crops they grew went directly to lords for taxes and dues. Why would they want to risk further reducing yields with unfamiliar methods that had no guarantee of success?

So peasants continued to farm as they had farmed since the Middle Ages. Many had no plows, and instead used hoes and spades to break up the soil. Because teams of oxen or horses were expensive, a farmer lucky enough to own a plow often harnessed it to his wife, or to several of his children. Peasants grew mostly grain, which could be dried and stored against the threat of famine, but growing grain was terribly hard on the soil. So much did grain crops deplete the soil, in fact, that fields had to be "rested" for a full year every other growing season. Historians estimate that in some places in France half of the farmland was lying fallow at all times.

"The Number of Our Children Plunges Us into Despair"

Considering the problems with farming, the French people were lucky for many years. Weather and harvests were good until 1770, when a series of bad harvests began. This decline in agriculture coincided with a population explosion in France. Between 1770 and 1790, the population increased by two million, a predicament that made the food shortage that much more catastrophic.

With less food, the life of the peasant was even more difficult. Families could no longer get by on subsistence farming. "The number of our children plunges us into despair," stated a peasant grievance list in 1789. "We do not have the means to feed or clothe them; many of us have eight and nine children."[27]

Large families put a strain on housing, too. Peasants' homes were all the same—damp walls of clay and straw, thatched roof, cold and dark inside because there were no windows. The floor was trampled-down earth, and the dank smell of mildewed walls competed with the stink of urine from the manure pile outside the front door. The small house contained only one room—privacy was a luxury no peasant could afford.

It is not hard to understand why many peasants sought additional jobs to earn more

This cartoon uses the fable of the spider and the fly to satirize the relationship between the noble and the peasant. The noble sits idly waiting for the peasant to give the noble his livelihood.

Never Enough Bread

Many historians maintain that the lack of bread was one of the chief causes of the French Revolution, that if the people had been well fed, no violence would have broken out among the common people. In her book, The Rights of Man, the Reign of Terror, *Susan Banfield describes the difficulties bakers endured in getting enough bread to the people of Paris.*

"Bakers . . . did backbreaking work—and for scant reward. Many had customers who bought on credit and did not pay their debts. Itinerant bakers had to contend with a law that forbade them to take out at the end of the day any bread they had brought in [to the city to sell] that morning. This meant they were frequently forced to sell their wares cheaply at closing time. Bakers were often in debt.

The production and sale of bread was a major preoccupation of the Paris police. There were rules governing which bakers were allowed to make rolls and which fine wheat bread. There were rules saying which grade of bread could be sold by the loaf (only white) and which grades had to be sold by weight (the brownish-white and brown breads eaten by the common people). There was the rule, already mentioned, forbidding itinerant bakers to leave the city with any of the bread they had brought in that morning. All of these had to be enforced. In addition, the police were responsible for monitoring the weight and quality of bread sold, a responsibility they took very seriously."

money. Just to pay the taxes levied against them, they took jobs as weavers, laborers, ditch diggers—anything to earn a few extra livre.

Opportunity in the Cities

When life in the countryside became too frightening, when starvation was too imminent a prospect, peasants moved to the larger towns and cities. Peasants sought out the increased opportunities to learn a trade or make money. And while the poor in the cities paid the same taxes as the rural peasants, at least there they escaped the indignities and penalties of the feudal system. Many peasants stayed on their farms only during planting and harvesting, living in the city most of the year. As one writer reported in 1769, "The only industry [job opportunity] the inhabitants [of poor rural areas] have is to leave home for nine months of the year." [28]

Of course, there was plenty to fear in the cities, too. They were filthy, overcrowded places, at least where the poor lived. Food was often rancid and the water supply was contaminated by human waste. Lice and rats, which spread disease, were everywhere. The death rate in the towns and cities was so high, say historians, that a steady stream of peasants from the country was needed to replenish the ranks of urban laborers and tradesmen.

But even with disease, rats, and foul water, peasants did have a fighting chance in the cities. There were, after all, institutions in the cities whose purpose was to assist the homeless and feed the hungry, a sort of safety net provided until a peasant family could find work. "In towns immigrants could find monasteries and convents distributing alms," writes one historian, "hospitals and poor houses endowed to take in and relieve those no longer able to fend for themselves, and more chance of private charity than in . . . villages where everyone was as poor as themselves."[29]

Ironically, however, such places were vigorously opposed by the aristocracy. It was their opinion that poorhouses and shelters for the homeless and ill were actually hurting France, for they encouraged idleness and laziness among the poor. If the priests and nuns would stop coddling the shiftless, they felt, the poor would soon learn that they could not depend on handouts.

"No One Was Ashamed to Beg"

There was another option for those who were starving and had no job. In France in the late 1700s about 10 percent of the people were beggars, doing nothing but moving from city to town to rural village asking for help. As one parish priest wrote in 1774, the millions of beggars even included those who had jobs, but whose families were starving anyway. It was a cycle of poverty that was repeated from generation to generation.

Day laborers, workmen, journeymen, and all those whose occupation does not provide for much more than food and clothing are the ones who make beggars. As young men they work, and when by their work they have got themselves decent clothing and something to pay their wedding costs, they marry, raise a first child, have much trouble in raising two, and if a third comes along their work is no longer enough for food, and the expense. At such a time they do not hesitate to take up the beggar's staff and take to the road.[30]

Not only fathers begged; whole families traveled together. Begging was so common,

A traveler is stopped in a small village by many of the town's inhabitants who have been reduced to begging. The hungrier and more desperate the Third Estate became, the greater their anger and resentment toward the nobility.

writes one expert, that there was no stigma attached to it. Begging was simply the way one earned his or her living. "No one was ashamed to beg. Fathers of large families had no qualms about sending their children out 'to earn their bread.' It was a trade like any other."[31]

Successful begging was an art form, and many used clever techniques to enhance their chance of success. Some faked blindness or wrapped yards of bandages around nonexistent wounds. Others found that a more aggressive approach produced better results. These people followed anyone who looked wealthy, calling and beseeching them in loud voices to share their good fortune. "Anything that made the better off pay up," writes one historian, "was worth trying. When appeals to pity failed, intimidation worked better, and from there it was a very short step to crime."[32]

Prostitution was a very common crime among the poor in prerevolutionary France, as was burglary and extortion. One of the most successful crimes was smuggling, for consumer items were taxed so many times during their transport around France that they were far too expensive for all but the most wealthy families. Anyone who could smuggle such goods across provincial borders and could avoid those taxes and duties would find a ready market, and be well paid for the risk.

"We Cannot Go to Bed Unafraid"

The sheer numbers and perseverance of the millions of beggars in France was frightening. Many people—especially other poor people—tried to help by sharing a crust of bread or a bowl of watery soup. But there were simply too many beggars, and even some of those dedicated to helping the poor became alarmed.

In one rural district, priests urged government officials to "put a stop to the incursions of this great gang of people who trail about with a pack on their backs and crowds of children—and their mothers—who are never away from our doors and even manage to get inside our houses."[33]

Beggars were a serious problem in the countryside. Farmers were afraid that they would be hurt if they didn't (or couldn't) offer money or food to the groups of beggars. Everyone seemed to know someone who had been beaten, or whose wife had been sexually assaulted, or whose children had been threatened by such beggars. And all knew that even if they avoided a direct attack, almost certainly some anonymous vandalism—fruit trees cut down, fences torn down, cattle stabbed or mutilated, a barn set on fire—would follow a refusal to give alms.

Most frightening were the groups of beggars that came at night or in the early hours before the sun came up. As one farmer wrote: "About a dozen arrived in the early hours of Thursday morning. We have much to fear during the month of August. . . . We cannot go to bed unafraid; we are much troubled by the night-time beggars, not to mention those who come in the daytime in great numbers."[34]

But the peasants' pleas for protection were unanswered, just as were the pleas of the hungry and those seeking relief from their financial burdens. The sharp lines separating the haves and the have-nots in France were becoming wider and deeper. As they did, frustration gradually turned to resentment, which soon turned to rage.

CHAPTER 3

The Seeds of Revolution

Presiding over the three estates of French society—and the problems of each—was the monarchy. For eight hundred years, royalty had ruled France. Louis XVI was young, twenty years old, when he succeeded his grandfather, Louis XV, to the throne. The young man was the symbol of power, the embodiment of God's law in the kingdom. Unfortunately, his future would be a short one, for his ability to lead was woefully inadequate.

An Ordinary Man

Physically, Louis was not an imposing figure, although at five feet seven inches he was considered tall for that day. He was stout and tended to be clumsy, so that when he walked he seemed to waddle. He was nearsighted, which sometimes put him at a disadvantage when receiving dignitaries at court. "He thus seemed perpetually surprised, at a loss," writes historian Olivier Bernier, "but he refused to wear glasses on the grounds that they did not look dignified."[35]

But his behavior was often less than dignified, and Louis was sometimes the object of ridicule among the courtiers. He fell asleep during the entertainment at dinner, or during the long speeches of his ministers and advisers. Sometimes, said witnesses, he awoke with a jump, and seemed confused and in a stupor. He enjoyed practical jokes and physical humor; one writer reports that Louis sometimes "reverted to outright childishness,

playing pranks on his pages or roughhousing with them."[36]

But he was an honest man who felt genuine concern for his fellow human beings. He had no interest in being king. In fact, when his grandfather died, making Louis XVI the new king (his father and older brothers having died as well), members of the court found him and his young queen "embracing and kneeling, their faces awash with tears; and just as the doors opened, they were heard to say, 'Protect us, O God, we are too young to reign.'"[37]

Although more compassionate toward the unfortunate than his predecessors, Louis XVI was a weak leader.

Being king was difficult work for which Louis lacked both interest and ability. As one historian writes:

> He never bothered to hide the fact that affairs of state bored him, and the virtues of Louis the man often proved to be vices in Louis the politician. His amiability became indecision; his honesty made him narrow-minded and incapable of compromise; his shyness made him hard to reach. He did not understand people, and his lack of judgement led him to rely on untrustworthy counselors. He found it difficult to concentrate on the dull business of government, and when a decision was forced on him, he frequently wavered, torn by the opposing views of the advisers on whom he depended.[38]

Bored by affairs of state, Louis spent happy hours hunting in the royal forests and puttering in his workshop, making and repairing locks. One who knew the king once remarked that "Nature had made [him] an honorable man, who would have done well in some obscure station."[39] It was his bad luck to have been thrust by accident of birth into an extraordinarily powerful position in extraordinarily difficult times.

Queen Marie Antoinette

Quite commonly a weak or indecisive ruler is vulnerable to manipulation by those around him, and Louis was no exception. Interestingly, the person who most influenced the king was not a minister, adviser, or courtier—it was, rather, his wife, Queen Marie Antoinette.

She was as young as her husband when they assumed the throne of France. She had come to France at age fourteen from her native Austria, and her marriage to Louis had been arranged by her mother, the empress Maria Theresa, as a way of cementing political bonds between the two nations.

At first, Marie was popular with the French people. She was elegant and beautiful, everything a queen should be. And she was everything her husband was not—purposeful, energetic, and ambitious. She was determined to assist her husband so that the monarchy in France would be a strong, vital one.

But she made enemies quickly. Many older members of the court disliked her impulsiveness and what seemed to them a lack of respect. She sometimes giggled at the wrong time or made faces to make one of her friends giggle. The irreverent young queen was headstrong and did not like being pushed into the background by the king's ministers and advisers, whose attitude was that she need not involve herself in politics anyway. What she should confine herself to, they believed, were the traditions and rules of etiquette that were so much a part of the monarchy.

The Levee

For the royal couple, no part of the day was without its rules of etiquette, most of which dated back to the time of the Middle Ages. The manner in which the king and queen ate, how they received guests, how they dressed on certain occasions—all involved strict rules, which monarchs followed for hundreds of years without question. Not Marie Antoinette. She found many traditions senseless and often ridiculous and was not afraid to say so.

At no time in Marie Antoinette's day was this etiquette more pronounced than at the *levee*, or rising in the morning. As queen, she had the attention of scores of handmaidens and attendants, each of whom had the privilege of performing some task for her. The tasks were small and rigidly sequential. One handed the queen her facecloth, one brought the warm water, another a brush for her hair, and so on. To make the process even more confusing, when a princess or blood relative walked in during the levee, an attendant was required to yield her task to the visitor. It is not hard to understand why it took almost two hours to wash and dress the queen each morning!

One of Marie Antoinette's ladies-in-waiting related an occasion during the levee in which the queen lost her patience with all of the little rules:

Marie Antoinette with one of her hairstyles—just one of the many ways that she influenced French fashion. Vain and self-centered, Marie enjoyed the public attention her appearance garnered.

One winter day the Queen, who was quite undressed, was about to put on her chemise [a light undershirt]. I was holding it unfolded; the Lady of Honor entered, hastily took off her gloves and took the chemise. There was a knock at the door, which was opened; it was the Duchess de Chartres. She took off her gloves and came forward to take the chemise, but the Lady of Honor could not present it to her. She gave it back to me and I gave it to the Princess. Another knock; it was the Countess de Provence; the Dutchess de Chartres handed her the chemise. The Queen held her chest and seemed to be cold. Madame noticed her discomfort and merely throwing aside her handkerchief kept on her gloves and in putting on the chemise disarranged the hair of the Queen, who began to laugh to conceal her impatience, but not without having muttered several times, "How odious! How annoying!"[40]

Big Hair and Prestige

But though Marie disliked many of the traditions associated with being queen, she did not dislike the prestige and the influence of her royalty. She derived particular pleasure from creating new and different styles for herself, and watched with glee as others imitated her.

She had her own physiognomist, a man whose sole job was to make sure her face revealed her beauty at all times. The man, whose name was Leonard, was given the task of designing new ways for Marie to wear her hair; he worked with her dressmaker to ensure that the queen's hair and fashions were always coordinated.

The results were nothing less than astonishing. Marie's hairstyle was the most unusual

An engraving satirizes the French nobility's penchant for big hair. Marie Antoinette even had small figurines that reenacted scenes placed in her hair.

anyone at court had ever seen. Leonard had swirled her hair upward, and teased and back-combed the hair until it stood high on her head. Unwilling to stop there, the queen asked if some innovative ornamentation could be arranged in her hair—different from jeweled bows or ribbons, that is.

Leonard's answer was to place what he termed "sentimental scenes" in the queen's hairstyle. Writes one biographer:

> One day [she] might appear with a garden in her hair, complete with tiny summer houses, statues and flower beds. On another day a hunting party might be seen chasing a deer across her head. Or the scene might be of a country village with an amorous boy and girl lolling behind a [haystack].[41]

The innovation caused a sensation in court; soon almost all the women were wearing their hair in Marie's style. Historians say the fashion caused a few problems, however. Since coach ceilings of the day were quite low, women wearing their hair in this new style were forced to travel with their heads out the windows. And doorways throughout the fashionable parts of France had to be raised so the queen and her look-alikes could pass through them more easily.

A Monument to Wealth and Power

The royalty of France made their home in Versailles, a town twelve miles west of Paris. The palace there was almost beyond description. Originally a royal hunting lodge, Louis XIV had it expanded and rebuilt it before moving his court there in 1685 from the busy city of Paris. It was, without a doubt, one of the wonders of Europe.

Not only the king and queen lived at Versailles; dukes, earls, relatives of the king and queen, and many other high-ranking officials had apartments there, with separate offices and their own staffs of servants. More than ten thousand people lived or worked in the palace. It was, says one historian, "a riot of halls and galleries, apartments and state rooms, terraces and courtyards."[42]

Here there were ballrooms, elegant throne rooms, hundreds of suites and bedrooms, even rooms for the king's favorite hunting dogs. There were 2,000 horses in the

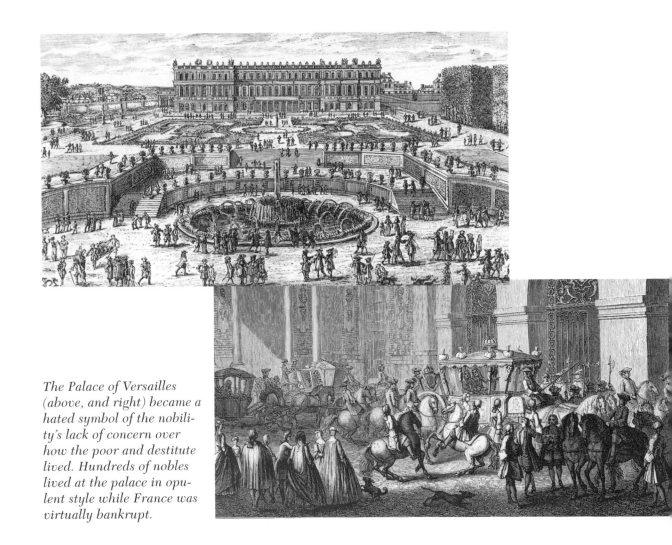

The Palace of Versailles (above, and right) became a hated symbol of the nobility's lack of concern over how the poor and destitute lived. Hundreds of nobles lived at the palace in opulent style while France was virtually bankrupt.

palace stables, with 1,500 men employed as groomsmen. There were dog kennels and large areas reserved for the royal falcons. The lavish lawns and gardens included 250 acres of emerald green grass, shrubs, and manicured flower beds. Groves of trees grew everywhere, and scores of fountains sparkled and glittered.

Favored by the King

According to tradition, any well-dressed person could visit the palace; however, it was not that easy to see the king. Those who spoke face-to-face with the king of France were part of an elite group called "Honors of the Court." This was the cream of the nobility—the king's hunting comrades whose pedigrees showed noble ancestry dating back to the year 1400.

But as glorious a place as the palace at Versailles was, many nobles who could have lived there did not. Only the wealthiest members of the aristocracy could afford the right clothes, the requisite servants and personal staffs, the upkeep of the apartment, and the costly entertainments that went along with palace life.

Granted, many of the courtiers were generously supported by the king, who had tens of millions of livres to lavish on his favorite, most trusted courtiers. (This was a practice begun by Louis XIV, who heaped large amounts of money on nobles in exchange for relinquishing their power in government.)

Historians note that most of the activities engaged in by the nobles were designed to please the king, to assure him of their support. Life at the palace was often more about gaining status and influence than it was about showing true loyalty; "having the king's ear" was more important than anything else. One of Marie Antoinette's ladies-in-waiting left a rather chilling description of the moment of Louis XV's death, indicating how quickly that king's courtiers were willing to switch their allegiance. In the palace that night, she wrote, "a terrible noise exactly like thunder was heard in the outer room of [the new king's] apartments: it was the crowd of courtiers deserting the antechamber of the dead sovereign to come and greet the new power of Louis XVI." [43]

The Palace at Versailles

Nowhere in Europe was there a more elegant residence than the famed palace at Versailles. As historian Susan Banfield writes in her book The Rights of Man, the Reign of Terror, *the palace was not only large, but astonishingly luxurious.*

"Viewed from the outside, Versailles' vast redbrick facades, hundreds of high, arched windows, and wide marble steps created an air of stately grandeur. The interior was more magnificent still.

The Hall of Mirrors, where Louis XVI received delegates to the Estates General, was three quarters the length of a football field and over forty feet high. It was decorated with rich marble, gilded sculpture, and more than three hundred Venetian mirrors. At night these reflected the light from fourteen silver and crystal chandeliers. For grand occasions the hall was lined with orange trees in silver tubs.

The Hall of Mirrors was just one of many grand salons that were used by the King for a variety of purposes. All were rich in marble, gilt, and statues sculpted by the most renowned artists of the time. The private rooms of the royal family were also imposing. Furniture was covered with enamel, silver, and gilt. High ceilings were decorated with masterpieces of the painters' art.

The grandeur of the palace was continued in its gardens. The elaborate formal gardens of Versailles covered 250 acres. They were crisscrossed by miles of straight, wide pathways and avenues bordered by precisely pruned hedges and rows of flowers planted just so. These pathways divided the gardens into dozens of small glens and groves. Each of these was decorated with special trees and statues to give it a unique appearance. Fourteen hundred fountains dotted the gardens."

A Financial Mess

It must have been difficult for those living amid the wealth and glitter of Versailles in the late 1700s to imagine that France was in financial straits. However, one look in the royal treasury would have told the story. The kingdom was teetering on the edge of bankruptcy. Of course, the fault was not all Louis XVI's; his predecessors had done their share of spending, too.

A series of military campaigns France waged between 1730 and 1783 was the main reason for the economic crisis. The most expensive of these were fought in North America: the French and Indian War and the assistance to the American colonies in their fight against England during the American Revolution. The wars were financed by loans but the government in the late 1780s could not make payments on those loans. There seemed to be no alternative but to borrow more money to pay them off.

But military expenses weren't the only reason for the kingdom's financial mess. The ridiculously extravagant lifestyle of the monar-

"Something Was Changing"

In his book Words of Fire, Deeds of Blood, *historian Olivier Bernier describes the economy of France in the 1780s. A land whose wealth had always come from farming, France was beginning to develop some industries. This was important to the French people, both in terms of what they did for a living, and of how much they made at it.*

"There had always been workshops in which artisans made furniture or cloth or tableware of extraordinary quality; but in the last two decades [before 1789] a number of larger manufacturing concerns had been set up in the eastern suburbs of Paris, the Faubourgs Saint-Antoine and Saint-Marcel. . . . The employers ranged from the Reveillon wallpaper factory, with its 350 workers, to the Santerre brewery, with 100 workers, to family businesses employing four or five men, and it was among these varied manufacturers that unemployment was spreading. There was, of course, no planned assistance for the families of jobless men, and their wages were, at the best of times, so small that they could not conceivably save against a rainy day.

A man of all work, in 1789, made 30 *sous* [a *sou* was the modern equivalent of 25 cents] a day, a mason 40, a carpenter 50. Against this must be set their expenses: a four-pound loaf of bread usually cost 8 to 9 *sous,* but in bad times could go as high as 20. Bread alone normally took up half a man's wages; vegetables, fats, and wine another 16 percent; clothes 15 percent, with the balance, 19 percent, spent on rent and incidentals.

Obviously, it was a hard life: observing normal religious holidays, laborers could expect to work no more than 250 days a year. Thus a carpenter might make about 625 *livres* to keep himself and his family in a world where, at the other extreme, the King and the royal family were spending 30 million a year."

chy also was a key factor. Some of the traditions and customs of the court were easy to abolish, and Louis did so. For instance, a new king traditionally exacted a tax of forty million livres when he assumed the throne. Called the "tax of joyous succession," it was like a coronation present that the public had no choice but to give. Realizing the people were already overtaxed, Louis had refused the "joyous succession" tax. However, there were many costly customs and privileges that the king and queen did not refuse, and these were painfully obvious to the common people.

"Madame Deficit"

The most visible spender in the court was Marie Antoinette. Everyone seemed to have heard of her outrageous spending. Her wardrobe, for instance, was legendary, and the common people grumbled that it was she who was singlehandedly bleeding the treasury dry.

Each year the queen was given an allowance for shoes, jewels, and clothing, an allowance she routinely insisted needed to be increased. She bought nearly one hundred dresses each year, for all sorts of occasions. At the end of the year, all the dresses were discarded; some of them had never been worn.

The same attitude applied to the queen's royal apartments. Hundreds of candles were used to light her rooms, and custom dictated that they be extinguished and discarded every time she left a room. Even brand-new candles that had burned for less than ten minutes were replaced for no practical reason. Candles worth hundreds of dollars were used each day, which when given to the queen's ladies-in-waiting to sell, netted them an annual income of over fifty thousand livres.

Marie Antoinette was generally hated in France both for her Austrian heritage and for her profligate spending. Marie continually demanded increases in her generous clothing allowance, which she used to buy over one hundred dresses a year.

But lavish wardrobes and new candles were traditional and accepted luxuries of the court. The queen's love of gambling was not—especially when Louis was forced to pay her gambling debts, totaling almost a half million livres. Nor was the queen's personal getaway, a retreat called Le Petit Trianon.

Beginning in 1782 the queen began fixing up the country retreat, paying a small fortune for Le Petit Trianon to resemble a little country village, complete with peasants' cottages, pastures, mills, and barns. "To make the cottages and other buildings look old," writes one historian, "the chimneys were made black with smoke, and cracks

Le Petite Trianon, the country home that Marie Antoinette spent a small fortune remodeling to have it resemble a self-containing country village. Although France's financial troubles were not caused by Marie alone, she was the most unabashed in her spending.

were painted on the beams and boards. The milk pails, instead of being wooden buckets, were of the finest Sevres porcelain and decorated with the queen's monogram."[44] Even the sheep were sanitized, with blue silk ribbons and silver bells around their laundered necks. When life at court became too dull, Marie and her friends could dress up as country milkmaids and watch servants milk cows.

With such glaring differences between the poverty of the common people and the unbridled spending of the queen, it is not hard to understand why people spoke angrily of her. They called her "Madame Deficit" and wondered why the king, who seemed to be a decent man, could not control the lavish appetites of his wife. Certainly Marie Antoinette was not the sole reason for the lack of money in the treasury; however, in a land where the majority of people lived lives of poverty, they complained, why should she have millions of livres to throw away?

The Nobles Say No

As the financial crisis worsened, Louis tried desperately to find solutions. Financial ministers urged him to borrow more money to repay loans, but everyone recognized that as a stopgap measure. Something had to be done to increase revenues. Taxes were already high; the common people could take no more.

The most obvious answer was also a very unpopular one—tax the nobility and clergy. If they paid their share, debts would be more than repaid and France would be on its way to solvency once more. Predictably, however, the nobles refused to consider the idea. Having lost so much political power over the years, they were utterly unwilling to lose their tax-exempt status, too.

But the situation in 1787 was desperate, and Louis knew that he had to do something quickly. He considered approaching the *parlements*, a group of thirteen courts that sat in regions throughout France. The *parlements* had been around for many centuries, although their power had diminished over the years. Still, a royal decree had to be registered with the courts to become law. But the *parlements* were composed of nobles, who would be unwilling to go along with any proposal that would take away their tax-exempt status.

Instead, Louis called on another aristocratic body, one comprising 144 of the most important men in France. Called the Assembly of Notables, its members told the king that assessing taxes more equally upon the three

The marquis de Lafayette, a famed war hero, recommended to the king that he call a meeting of the Estates General to solve the taxation issue.

estates of France would not be acceptable to them. One of the assembly's most famous members, the marquis de Lafayette, who had gained fame for his heroic exploits in America in the war against England, had a suggestion for the king. Lafayette urged Louis to convene another esteemed body, the Estates General, which could perhaps help him pass such radical tax measures.

The Estates General, like the *parlements,* was a holdover from the Middle Ages, a time when the king held less power. The Estates General was similar to the British Parliament or the American Congress. It was made up of delegates from all three estates, not just aristocrats. Over the centuries, however, as the monarchy's power increased, the Estates General lost all its influence. Even though it was still legally a functioning body, it had not convened in 174 years!

The King Says No

But Louis did not want the Estates General to convene. He had reigned for thirteen years without the assistance of that body and he had no interest in appealing to them now, in the spring of 1788. Angrily he went back to the *parlement* of Paris, the largest and most influential of the regional courts. Would it do His Majesty's bidding, and allow a new tax reform measure to be made into law?

The *parlement* refused. Nobles who sat on that court were annoyed with the king for trying to circumvent them by appealing first to the Assembly of Notables. Historians say that Louis became so angry at the "impudence of the *parlement*" that he ordered two of its members arrested and the rest exiled to the small town of Troyes. In addition, he decreed that all other regional *parlements* be disbanded.

Louis's angry actions against the *parlements* had dire consequences. Throughout France, there was a storm of loud and sometimes violent protest from furious citizens. How dare the king disband their courts? Never mind that these were courts staffed entirely by nobles—they were still the only true link with power that each region of France had.

Ironically perhaps, the common people felt sympathy for the nobles of the *parlements*, who were being bullied by a powerful king. The fact that the nobles were fighting for their tax-exempt status and had no interest whatever in the common people's plight did not keep the commoners from backing the *parlements*. Visitor Arthur Young was a witness to some of the violence during the spring of 1788. Although he recognized the common people had much to be angry about, it confused him that they should be so active on behalf of the nobles. "The discontents of the people have been double," he wrote. "First on account of the high price of bread, and secondly for the banishment of the *parlement*. The former cause is natural enough but why the people should love their *parlement* is what I could not understand."[45]

Throughout France government officials, ordered to force the courts to disband, were attacked with sticks and stones. In Grenoble, police closing the *parlement* there were showered with heavy stones thrown from the rooftops of buildings by angry crowds; that day became known as the "Day of Tiles."

No Choice for King Louis

King Louis now had a potentially dangerous situation on his hands. An alliance between the nobles and the common people against the monarchy would upset the balance of French society. It was clear that Louis needed to do something quickly to defuse the anger of the people.

He chose to allow the Estates General to meet—in Versailles, he told an aide, not in Paris, for he had no intention of missing his hunting on account of such meetings. The nobles were jubilant, as one historian relates:

> To [them] it seemed as if victory were close at hand. They had had their way with the king. They also felt confident that when the Estates General convened, that body would usher in an era of reform that would crush the king's absolute power, and would restore to their order the power it had enjoyed in days of old.[46]

The king, sullen because he had had to make concessions to the people that he had not intended making, hoped that this would be the end of the conflict. In a royal proclamation announcing his decision to convene the Estates General, he wrote:

> His Majesty is already looking forward to calm and peaceful days after the storm, to seeing order restored in all the provinces, to the national debt being consolidated and to France enjoying, without disturbance, the power and respect due to its size, population, wealth, and the character of its people.[47]

Neither the smug nobility nor King Louis XVI knew that "the storm" had not yet begun—and that before it was over they would all be exiled, imprisoned, or dead.

The Revolution Begins

The Estates General was scheduled to convene on May 5, 1789. Louis had instructed the people in each district to meet in advance and write out any grievances they had, to be compiled into lists and presented by various representatives when the Estates General met.

"We Beg His Majesty to Have Pity"

As so few peasants could read or write, the lists, known as *cahiers*, were often composed by a group of men (women were not consulted) while standing outside the church on a Sunday, with the most literate doing the actual writing. Even so, the finished products were often illegible, and filled with mysteries of spelling and punctuation. But historians say that the cahiers give a vivid picture of what life was really like for the peasants who comprised the majority of France.

One list, from the village of Menouville, is very specific about the hardships of farming. "We beg His Majesty to have pity on our farmland," it begins,

> because of the hail we have had. Also we have a great deal of waste land which is covered with juniper, and this causes much trouble on account of the rabbits which are very numerous; it is this that makes us unable to pay the dues we owe to His Majesty. . . . We have only a few good fields very remote from the village, the rest is wretched land very full of game and this causes very small harvests.[48]

Another cahier, from the village of Bourscheid, complains about the many dues and taxes the peasants there are forced to pay the nobles who own the land. "The undersigned inhabitants believe they should begin their *cahier* by giving an idea of the different dues they pay. . . . They pay one hen per year per household. Each household must spin annually two pounds of flax or three of hemp. . . . Each farmer pays annually on plowland, whether the land is sown or not."[49]

Excitement in the Air

The Third Estate had requested a change in the traditional way of selecting delegates to the Estates General. Since they were obviously the most populous group in France, why was it that they had only three hundred delegates—the same number as the nobility and clergy?

Louis's finance minister, Jacques Necker, believed that it made good political sense for the king to grant the request of the Third Estate for proportional representation. After all, by ingratiating himself with the common people, Louis would surely drive a wedge between them and the nobility, undermining an alliance that was making Louis nervous.

Necker and the king agreed to the request, doubling the number of delegates that would represent the Third Estate. It was, as Necker had predicted, a smart move. "Almost overnight," writes one historian, "the king and his minister became popular idols."[50] Whether the voting would be done by head count or by the traditional method in which each estate received one vote remained unclear, however. The common people were optimistic; persuaded that Louis was on their side, they believed things would work in their favor.

The Power of the Press

Nowhere in France was excitement more intense than in Paris. The topic of the upcoming Estates General assembly seemed to be on everyone's mind; one could not stroll the boulevards or go to a coffeehouse or a tavern without hearing heated political arguments. What would—or should—the Estates General accomplish? Would the king allow the kind of sweeping reforms the Third Estate was asking for?

Arthur Young visited Paris in the spring of 1789 and observed the debates firsthand.

> The coffeehouses in the Palais-Royal present yet more singular and astonishing spectacles: they are not only crowded within, but other expectant crowds are at the doors and windows, listening . . . to certain orators, who from chairs and tables harangue each his little audience. The eagerness with which they are heard, and the thunder of applause they receive for every sentiment of more than common hardiness or violence against the present government cannot be easily imagined.[51]

Jacques Necker, King Louis's finance minister, convinced the king that increasing the Third Estate's representation in the Estates General would drive a wedge between the people and the nobility—which could only help the king.

Pamphlets and newsletters played a large part in the political uproar, too; there seemed to be more editorials being published than one could count. One newcomer wrote:

> I went to . . . see what new things were published and to procure a catalog of all. Every hour produces something new. Thirteen came out today, sixteen yesterday, and ninety-two last week. . . . One can scarcely squeeze from the floor to the counter. . . . Nineteen twentieths of these productions are in favor of liberty, and commonly violent against the clergy and nobility.[52]

Some of the editorials were tracts on political ideology in general. A great many echoed the ideas of Jean-Jacques Rousseau, a philosopher and writer whose work strongly influenced the political thinking of the day. Rousseau believed that only when government ruled according to the wishes and interests of the people was its existence justified. He also believed that kings derived their power to rule not from God, as French tradition declared, but from the consent of the people.

On the other hand, many pamphlets addressed very specific or practical issues that would be set before the Estates General.

One writer, a clergyman named Sieyes, created a stir with a pamphlet called *What Is the Third Estate?* Sieyes argued that the delegates representing the Third Estate in the Estates General were the only true representatives of the people of France. He wrote:

We have three questions to ask ourselves. What is the Third Estate? EVERYTHING. What has it been in the political order until now? NOTHING. What is it asking for? To become SOMETHING. Who would dare to say that the Third

The Center of Paris Life

Nowhere in Paris was there a more active, thriving area than the Palais Royal, where people gathered to shop, eat, drink, discuss politics, and simply mingle. The evening scene at the Palais Royal is remembered by one witness in Elizabeth Wormeley Latimer's book My Scrap-Book of the French Revolution.

"But the real center of Parisian life in 1789 I know to be the Palais Royal. It is nine o'clock in the evening, and in spite of the non-discovery of gas, or of electricity, the Palais Royal is a blaze of light from one end to the other. Under the arcades jewellers display their wares behind the little panes of their narrow windows which glitter like the stars. Here are long chains of jewels, pearls, and precious stones; watches by wholesale, rings of all kinds; diamond or rhinestone earrings, snuff-boxes, . . . and gold, silver, or enamelled cups of antique shapes with ebony handles. The drapers and mercers have rich stuffs hanging from the ceiling to the floor of their establishments, and those who pass by finger them—not always with clean hands.

There are restaurants, cafes, and eating stands. Drinking and eating go on at all hours, street musicians are endeavoring to charm those who are sitting at dinner, and beggars are imploring charity with a nasal whine.

In the gardens and under the arcades lounge a singular and promiscuous crowd. Dandies dressed in silk elbow vagabonds swarming with vermin. An English family all agape with curiosity has encountered a party of Turks, wearing enormous turbans, who pretend to take no interest in anything around them.

Young men of fashion sit on chairs at their ease in the garden, staring at the women through their glasses, eating ices and reading the gazettes, for the place is as bright as day. The news of the past 24 hours is discussed. There are disputes and quarrels and reconciliations."

Estate does not have in itself all that is needed to form a complete nation? It is a man who is strong and robust but still has one arm in chains. Take away the privileged order, and the nation would not be less, but more.[53]

Dashed Hopes

But when the Estates General convened with grand opening ceremonies on May 5, 1789, it appeared that the hopes and expectations of the common people and their delegates were too high. In fact, there seemed to be a real effort on the part of the king and the nobility to embarrass the Third Estate delegates, to treat them as less important than the delegates from the First and Second Estates.

For example, the style of dress that was dictated for all delegates accentuated the differences within the estates. The clergy marched in wearing brilliant ceremonial robes, capes of purple and turquoise and red silk, and velvet trim. The nobles wore gold-embroidered silks, colorful capes, and plumed hats, and gleaming swords flashed at their sides. The delegates of the Third Estate, in contrast, wore dull black coats and black stockings.

It was time for each estate to present its lists of grievances to the king. Louis sat in the breathtakingly beautiful Hall of Mirrors in the palace as the delegates from the nobility and clergy filed by. However, Louis did not want to meet the Third Estate in the Hall of Mirrors, preferring instead to keep the commoners waiting until he moved to a less luxurious room. "There, after he kept them waiting for three hours, he had the delegates of the common people file past him," writes historian Susan Banfield. "There was a deep silence as the gentlemen in black slowly walked past, for the king said not so much as a 'good morning' to any of them, save one older gentleman who looked fairly harmless."[54]

Neither Louis nor the nobility and clergy would allow the Estates General to vote by

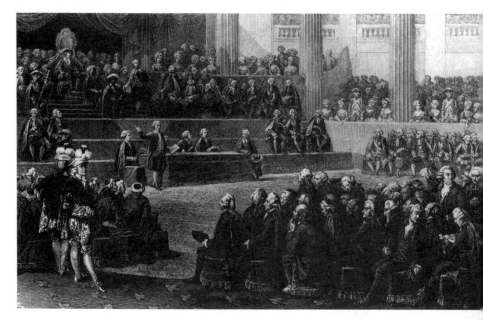

The meeting of the Estates General in 1789. The meeting was protested by members of the Third Estate, who were at first excluded from meeting in the same room as members of the clergy and nobility.

The Grand Procession

The opening ceremonies of the convening of the Estates General on May 5, 1789, were a colorful religious pageant. The marquis de Bombelles, one of the court aristocrats, described the spectacle in a journal entry quoted by Richard Cobb in Voices of the Revolution.

"A brilliant day having succeeded the heavy rain that had fallen all night, King Louis XVI, accompanied by a splendid retinue, made his way to the parish church of Notre-Dame, in Versailles. Two rich banners went ahead of the Recollects, who were followed by the clergy of one of the two parishes of Versailles. Next came the three orders of deputies. The archbishop of Paris carried the Holy Sacrament, and then came the king.

The bodyguards . . . were on duty at this church. The prayer stool for the king and queen, the chairs, all the seats for the royal family and their retinue, as well as the vast canopy suspended from the vault, were of purple velvet or satin strewn with gold-embroidered fleurs de lis.

The benches on the right were for the clergy, those on the left for the nobility, and places were reserved for the Third Estate near the choir. All these benches were taken indiscriminately, just as the Third Estate felt inclined; they then refused point blank to give them up to the nobility.

Once the king had arrived, mass began. The bishop of Nancy, deputy of the clergy, preached. Sermon and mass done, the king went back to the palace of Versailles by carriage, as did the queen. There were frequent shouts of 'Long live the king!'; those of 'Long live the queen!' were half-hearted. No queen of France has been less liked."

head, as the commoners had hoped. Doubling the number of delegates for the Third Estate had been an empty gesture on Louis's part, one that would have no significance here. It was clear to the delegates of the Third Estate that they had no chance of voting in reforms through this assembly.

The National Assembly Is Born

After the opening ceremonies, each delegation went off to a separate room to work. It was the clergyman Sieyes who finally proposed to the six hundred frustrated delegates of the Third Estate that they declare themselves the official representative body of France. Whether their declaration was "allowed" by Louis and the nobles, said Sieyes, was not important. They must make a stand, and stand together.

They agreed, and on June 17 declared themselves with no small bravado the National Assembly, the true representative body of the French nation. The nobility and clergy could make no laws for France, they said. Not even the king could reject any decision made by the National Assembly. It was a bold move, popular with the crowds of people gathered outside the windows of the hall, hoping for some word of progress. But what would be the reaction of the king and the aristocracy?

Members of the Third Estate swear to remain united until they are allowed to draft a new constitution. Because they met in a building that housed the royal tennis courts, the oath was called the Tennis Court Oath.

They did not wait long for an answer. A few days later the new assembly came to their chamber to meet, and found the door locked and guarded. The soldier told the delegates that the chamber was undergoing construction, but the delegates knew better. Louis was preventing them from meeting, at least until he could decide how to deal with this defiant assembly.

"Tell Your Master"

But the assembly would not be disbanded. They went to a nearby indoor tennis court and began excited deliberations there. They vowed that they would not disperse until they had drafted a constitution for the new government they envisioned for France.

It was a bold step, and a provocative one, met with hostility from Louis. He warned the assembly that what they were doing was illegal and dangerous, saying, "Not one of your projects, not one of your resolutions can have force of law except by my special consent. I order you to separate immediately."[55]

The king quickly left the court after delivering his stern warning. None of the delegates to the National Assembly made a move to leave. In fact, several members of

the clergy joined them there. And when a royal deputy returned to repeat the order more forcefully, several of the soldiers with him turned their backs. They would not use force on these commoners.

A spokesman for the assembly shouted at the deputy that they were not intimidated by threats from the king. "Tell your master that we are assembled here by the will of the people," he announced, "and that we will leave only at the point of a bayonet!"[56]

The king had to admit defeat; there were not enough troops at his command to fight all of the delegates, let alone the thousands of commoners who cheered them on. Observers were impressed by the peacefulness of the event—a government had changed hands without a shot being fired. American Thomas Jefferson, who was U.S. minister to France at the time, wrote:

> The National Assembly . . . having shown through every stage . . . a coolness, wisdom, and resolution to set fire to the four corners of the kingdom and to perish with it themselves rather than to relinquish an iota from their plan of a total change of government, are now in complete and undisputed possession of sovereignty.

He continued:

> The executive and the aristocracy are now at their feet: the mass of the nation, the mass of the clergy, and the army are with them. They have prostrated the old government, and are now beginning to build one from the foundation.[57]

Jefferson's sentiments were echoed by Arthur Young, who marveled that the courage of the National Assembly had forced such a concession, that the absolute monarchy of France was now a thing of the past. A new kind of government would rule in its place. "The whole business is now over," he wrote, "and the Revolution is complete!"[58]

The Hunger

For many of the common people, the political change occurring in Versailles was happy news. However, for most of the poor—rural peasants and city dwellers alike—politics was not the top priority in July of 1789. Paris, as well as the countryside surrounding it, was starving to death.

There had been poor harvests throughout most of France in 1788, ruined by hailstones so big that they killed a large number of men and animals. Crops, especially grain, were ravished by storms. The harvest was not expected to improve in 1789.

In the summer of 1789, with this year's questionable yields not yet harvested and last year's meager stores almost used up, there was not much bread to be found. Because it was scarce, the price was high, so that only the wealthier people could afford it. At that time bread made up about 75 percent of an average person's diet. Yet in the summer of 1789 its price had doubled, now costing 90 percent of a person's income.

Crowds of people stood in line most of each day outside bakeries, hoping they would be lucky enough to find even a single loaf of bread. Most of the time those in the lines went away disappointed and angry. The hungry masses of people in Paris were coming closer and closer to panic.

The Masses Take Charge

Most government officials sympathized with the commoners in their districts. They tried to control prices so the scarcity of bread didn't result in prices that no one could afford. As historian William Doyle notes, this concern was not merely goodwill on the part of the officials. "In the case of Paris this was considered a matter of national importance: if the capital went hungry the stability of the state itself might be endangered."[59]

But such precautions were taken far too late. Violence was becoming increasingly common around Paris, as the threat of starvation loomed. The city's food supply was brought in each day from the surrounding countryside, and the grain convoys were often robbed by peasants en route. There were more and more instances of shopkeepers and bakers being robbed, beaten, and sometimes lynched by hungry mobs.

Many tollgates and customs posts were burned by peasants who did not want to see the price of bread rise any higher. As Doyle explains, "With the tollgates gutted there would be no duty to pay on incoming goods. In the crude reasoning of the mob, that was the quickest way to lower the price of bread."[60]

Indeed, the price was far too high already—bad news for the worker trying to feed his family and for the economy as a whole. With nearly every penny spent on bread, people had no money for other consumer goods, and the workers who depended on such markets were hurt. Unemployment was high, and expectations were increasingly low.

The Toll of Starvation

Arthur Young wrote of the effects of the extreme hunger and poverty he witnessed in the countryside in 1788 and 1789 as a result of the bread shortage. "An Englishman who has not travelled cannot imagine the figure made by infinitely the greater part of the countrywomen in France. This woman, at no great distance, might have been taken for sixty or seventy, her figure was so bent, and her face so furrowed and hardened by labor; but she said she was only twenty-eight."[61]

But besides the physical changes, the sunken eyes and sallow complexions that slow

Political change was not a primary concern for the poor, who were starving from lack of bread. Due to a shortage of wheat, bakeries (above) could not make enough bread, and doubled the price. Since bread made up 75 percent of the average poor person's diet, long lines ensued (right).

Louis XVI distributes alms among the poor during the terrible winter of 1788. Starvation drove the poor to become more disgruntled, angry, and violent.

starvation causes, there was a change as well in the emotions of the masses in Paris. The streets seemed to be increasingly filled with aimless, potentially violent groups of people. As one authority explains:

> It was still an ill-defined, unsure, inchoate mass, without real leaders, without real goals, but it knew well enough that it had been oppressed for centuries. It was no longer ready to starve obediently; it heard the liberals who claimed that all men were equal, but it was also discovering its own raw strength, its ability to impose its wants and to suppress, physically, by the use of violence, any opposition.[62]

The mobs were restless and angry. Like a keg of gunpowder, it seemed that the slightest spark could provoke an explosion. Interestingly, it was Louis himself that provided the spark.

Bringing in Troops

In July rumors flew on every street corner and in every coffeehouse that soldiers were on their way to Paris. The king himself had sent for the troops, went the rumors, but no one was quite certain why. Some claimed Louis had decided that the masses of commoners were becoming a threat, and wanted to kill them all. Those more loyal to Louis disagreed, saying that perhaps the troops were coming to scare away troublemakers.

Whatever the true circumstances, it soon was verified that soldiers were indeed surrounding the city. Many people had seen them. They were not French soldiers, however, for more and more native troops were deserting their posts and siding with the common people. Instead, German and Swiss soldiers—seventeen regiments in all—were coming to France. They were paid by the king and had no loyalty to the commoners.

They had been summoned by Louis as a means of forcibly disbanding the National Assembly which worked out of Paris. But though the king had publicly agreed to the show of force, privately he had strong misgivings. He had been subject to a great deal of pressure from the queen, as well as from many of the nobles and high clergy. The National Assembly was a slap in the face of the king, they told him. To recognize it is to undermine the security of all of France.

His military advisers had urged Louis to deal harshly with the assembly and the people who supported it. One promised that a little grapeshot "would disperse these argufiers and restore the absolute power which is going out, in place of the republican spirit which is coming in."[63] Another assured the king that eliminating the threat to the monarchy was so important that "if it is necessary to burn Paris, Paris will be burned."[64] Unable to resist such strong arguments, Louis finally agreed.

Days went by and people began to wonder aloud if the new National Assembly might be the target of Louis's military might. If it were so, what of the freedoms and concessions that the assembly had promised to work for? Would things go back to the way they were before? "As troop movement became common knowledge," writes French authority Olivier Bernier, "it seemed that there might well not be a constitution, or indeed a National Assembly, if the king had his way. . . . It seemed most likely that, in a moment of violence, Louis XVI would reach for the power he had lost."[65]

"To Arms! To Arms!"

As the threat of violence by the king's soldiers grew more real, tension among the masses in Paris peaked. The coffeehouses and taverns were always full, and the sentiment seemed far more angry than ever before. Then, on July 12, news reached Paris that the king had dismissed Jacques Necker, the finance minister who was so popular with the common people, and the city seemed to explode.

At the Palais Royal, where for months crowds had gathered to listen to political discussions and speeches, a furious mob was milling about. Someone screamed that the soldiers would be there any minute. Another shouted that the only hope was for the people to arm themselves, to fight back against the tyrants, the soldiers of the king. "To arms! To arms!" was the cry, as the mob spilled into the street in search of weapons.

Finding them was a challenge. Some groups broke into the storehouse of the old palace and found some old guns and a cannon. Some seized ammunition from a ship's hold. Some broke into shops and warehouses looking for more weapons. From the military hospital in Paris, the Invalides, came the biggest cache of all—thirty thousand muskets.

Two days later, at the Invalides, it was clear how large and powerful the mob was. J.B. Humbert, a watchmaker, described the bedlam that resulted when the mob rushed into the hospital.

> The crowd at the top of the stairs was so great that all those who were climbing up were pushed down again, and fell right down into the cellar. . . . In spite of this horrible tumble, the crowd persisted in going down the stairs, and as nobody could get up again, there was such a crush in the cellar that people were shrieking and gasping for breath.
>
> Many people had fainted, so all those in the cellar who were armed followed the advice someone gave and forced the unarmed crowd to turn and go back,

threatening them with the points of their bayonets. The advice succeeded, and as the crowd drew back in terror we took advantage of this moment to form a line and force the people up the stairs.[66]

Having secured the Invalides' weapons, the crowd cried for gunpowder to load them. Jubilant, they knew that just a few hundred yards away was the city's gunpowder supply—in the storeroom of a four-hundred-year-old prison called the Bastille.

A Symbol of Tyranny

The Bastille was well known to the people of Paris. It was a huge, foreboding structure with gray stone walls nine feet thick and gun towers ninety feet high. Like a castle in a fairy tale, it had drawbridges, a moat, and a

French citizens storm the courtyard of the Invalides hospital to obtain the weapons stored there. When they found little ammunition, they quickly moved on to the Bastille, where it was stored.

series of grim cells where prisoners were said to be tortured and beaten daily.

The Bastille had become a symbol of the oppressive government so despised by the French people. For hundreds of years, the Bastille was the place people were held when they were arrested by order of the king. Because France had an absolute monarchy, a single word from the king could send anyone to prison without trial. "Prisoners arrived, it was said, in carriages with drawn blinds," writes one historian, "and mystery surrounded much that went on inside."[67]

An often-repeated story about the Bastille concerned the *chambre des oubliettes,* a beautiful room of roses and candlelight. "A prisoner, brought before the sadistic governor, would be promised his liberty," explains another historian. "Then, at a given signal, the floor would open and the captive would hurtle down on to a wheel of knives and be slashed to pieces."[68]

As grim and foreboding as the Bastille was, and as strong as its walls were, the angry crowd was determined to get the gunpowder stored within. The elderly governor in charge of the Bastille, the marquis de Launay, was frightened of the crowds that moved through Paris. Recent disturbances had so unnerved him, in fact, that "at night he mistook the shadows of trees and other objects round him for enemies."[69] The crowd this night of July 14 looked like they were ready for a battle, and de Launay was terrified.

Victory for the Mob

At the Bastille's gates, the crowd demanded the gunpowder, and sent delegates in to meet with de Launay. He refused to surrender the ammunition, but was willing to withdraw

Soldiers at the Bastille defend themselves by firing on the mobs gaining access to the main gates during the storming of the Bastille.

the guns he had pointed at the crowd from the towers and atop the walls. When the mob used axes to open the main gates of the prison, however, the soldiers inside responded with gunfire. In a few hours, more than eighty attackers lay dead on the cobblestones outside the Bastille.

Although in less volatile circumstances negotiations such as those being carried out between de Launay and the common people might have been successful, the mob outside was tired of waiting. They were angry and their sheer numbers gave them courage. Not waiting to see what the negotiations would yield, they dragged their stolen cannon to the walls of the Bastille.

De Launay knew his fortress could not withstand cannon fire at such close range, and surrendered. But, it was too late. As de Launay gave the signal for his soldiers to lower

the drawbridge and open the gates, the mob, chanting, "No surrender! No surrender!" streamed inside.

It was a grisly climax to a very frightening episode. Three of the Bastille's guards were butchered by the mob although they too had surrendered. And de Launay suffered the cruelest fate of all. "Under heavy escort he was taken as far as the steps of the city hall, but there the crowd overwhelmed his protectors and cut his throat," writes one historian. "His head was hacked off and paraded through the streets on a pitchfork."[70]

Clearly the civilized, bloodless nature of the revolt Arthur Young had observed with the creation of the National Assembly was an illusion. The Revolution was just beginning. Before it was over, there would be a great deal more bloodshed; indeed, the streets of Paris would be stained red.

The Citizens Take Charge

With the fall of the Bastille, it was necessary for the king to once more admit defeat. He had insufficient military strength to fight off every commoner in Paris, and he knew that his French troops were not entirely on his side. Better, he thought, to lose gracefully; he ordered his troops to withdraw from Paris, and he brought Necker back as minister.

A Gesture of Goodwill

The nature of the Revolution had clearly changed. Although protest had started with the nobility and aristocracy, it then had shifted to the bourgeoisie. But now, with violence in the countryside and the storming of the Bastille, no one could doubt that the peasants and the urban poor were feeling their muscle. They were undeniably a force behind the Revolution.

Hoping to assuage the anger of the common people somewhat, Louis decided to journey to Paris. He would think of it as a goodwill mission, a show of unity as he publicly accepted the National Assembly and the will of the people. The people were, after all, his subjects, and most of them bore him no personal ill will. The French people had had kings as long as anyone could remember, and reverence, honor, and even love was almost instinctive. Louis may not have been the best ruler, but he was their king.

Just how beloved Louis was to the people was clear when his carriage arrived in Paris.

King Louis makes his way to Paris while crowds of citizens wearing cockades cheer as he moves through the streets.

All along the way there were citizens with the flower-shaped decorations called cockades on their hats. The red, white, and blue cockades had become the symbol of the Revolution in France. (Red and blue were the colors of Paris, and white symbolized Louis's heritage.)

One witness recorded that as the king entered Paris, there were cannons thundering salvos, crowds cheering, and even a key-to-the-city presentation by the new mayor, Bailly. "The King went very slowly so that the people and the militia could keep up with them," he wrote.

> First the people shouted, *"Vive la Nation!"* ["Long live the nation!"] then *"Vive la Nation et l'Assemblee Nationale!"* ["Long live the nation and the National Assembly!"] and finally they shouted, *"Vive le Roi et la Nation!"* ["Long live the king and the nation!"]. [The king] was presented with a red, white, and blue cockade like those of the citizens. Bailly spoke on the king's behalf, and said that His Majesty was mindful of nothing except the love of his people. The king himself was moved, and did not speak.[71]

Violence in the Countryside

The Revolution was having a marked effect in the cities. In Paris there was an air of excitement, for there changes were happening that people could see. A new National Guard—a sort of people's militia—was being organized in Paris, and one by one, revolutionary town councils were taking over many of the offices formerly held by the king's appointees.

But as exciting as life was in the cities, in the countryside it was frightening. Rumors abounded that the king had ordered thugs to kill the common people, and that bands of angry aristocrats were ready to take their revenge on those who supported the National Assembly and the Revolution. "Whispered tales of bands—and even armies—of brigands sent by nobles to attack peasant farms passed from village to village," writes one expert. "Some of these stories were even printed in local papers. Within a week of the Bastille's fall, violence had erupted all over France."[72]

However, the violence was not directed *at* the peasants, but rather *by* the peasants. Many villages chose not to wait for an attack. Feeling threatened, many of the peasants lashed out, choosing to be aggressors rather than victims. As one country priest who witnessed the violence reported, "When the inhabitants heard that everything was going to be different, they began to refuse to pay both tithes and dues, considering themselves so permitted, they said, by the new law to come."[73]

Many other peasants were far more forceful. They looted and burned the country estates of the lords, destroyed forests and fishponds and even hanged several of the nobles they could get their hands on. As Arthur Young wrote in his journal on July 27: "The mischiefs which have been perpetrated in the country . . . are numerous and shocking. Many chateaus have been burnt, others plundered, the [lords] hunted down like wild beasts, their wives and daughters ravished, their papers and titles burnt, and all their property destroyed."[74]

The Great Fear

Such fierce anger was the result of fear; in fact, this period of the French Revolution is referred to as the Great Fear. Ironically, the death and destruction occurring because of

"I'll Do It, Even If It Costs Me My Life"

The crowds that marched to Versailles to bring the king back to Paris were rowdy and angry. Many marchers had spoken of doing harm to the queen, whom they particularly disliked. However, Marie Antoinette's courage when faced with the mob prevented at least one attempt on her life, as recalled by one deputy present at Versailles. This excerpt is included in The French Revolution, *edited by Georges Pernoud and Sabine Flaissier.*

"Standing on a chair in front of [the queen] was the Dauphin, who, as he ruffled his sister's hair, kept saying, "Mama, I'm so hungry." The Queen with tears in her eyes, told him he must be patient and wait till the turmoil was over. . . . She took the Dauphin in her arms and got up hastily. Then someone came to tell her that the people were calling for her. She hesitated a moment. [National Guard captain] La Fayette explained that she had to show herself in order to calm the people. 'In that case,' she said with spirit, 'I'll do it, even if it costs me my life.'

Then, holding the hands of her two children, she advanced to the balcony. 'No children!' cried a man in the crowd, so the Queen handed over the Dauphin and [her daughter] to [the governess] and advanced on to the balcony alone. One of the conspirators aimed his piece at her, but, shocked at the enormity of the crime he had planned, he did not dare to consummate it."

the peasants' fear seemed to convince other peasants that the wild rumors were true. Bands of peasants vandalizing the homes of nobles were often mistaken for the brigands and thugs peasants had been warned about. Curls of smoke from the houses and forests set ablaze by the peasants could be seen for miles and fed the too-vivid imaginations of country people, who resorted to further violence, which increased peasants' fears, and so on.

There was another cyclical aspect to the Great Fear. Many nobles left France because they were afraid for their lives. (They joined the ranks of those who had left in disgust because of the concessions Louis had been forced to make to the common people.) These nobles were known as *émigrés*, and although the peasants were glad to be rid of them, their absence created all kinds of problems for the working poor, especially those in the city.

For example, many of the jobs held by the Third Estate depended on wealthy nobles, a class of people who had the money to buy the products and services that the commoners provided. "For thousands of Parisians, such as carriage-makers, jewelers, hair dressers, decorators, and domestic servants, had made their living by working for the aristocracy," writes historian Sarel Eimerl. "Inevitably, the flight of the *émigrés* had thrown these people out of work and . . . they were desperately short of money."[75]

The Great Fear took a large toll on the hungry. Peasants who should have been tending their flocks and harvesting their grain were instead dashing through the countryside destroying property. The transport of grain to the mills and bread to the cities was interrupted. This caused more food shortages in an already starving Paris; the only bread available was outrageously expensive, and destined only for the tables of the wealthy.

"A Night for Destruction and Public Happiness"

The panic and violence of the Great Fear subsided only when the new people's militia was sent out to the countryside to keep order. Then the National Assembly took action to prevent such a disaster from occurring again soon.

Meeting on the night of August 4, 1789, and worried that the violence in the countryside was escalating to a level that perhaps the militia could not control, the members of the National Assembly enthusiastically called for an end to the feudal system, which had produced so much frustration and anger in the peasants. No longer, they decreed, would peasants be slaves or helpless servants for rich lords. From that time forward, all farmers would have the opportunity to own the land they farmed. Also, equal taxation would rearrange the financial burden on the people, so that everyone, not just the commoners, would pay a fair share.

This burst of revolutionary spirit was unplanned; some historians say that the proceedings surprised the legislators themselves. Wrote Mayor Bailly of Paris:

> Never before have so many bodies and individuals voted such sacrifices at one time, in such generous terms and with such unanimity. This has been a night for destruction and public happiness. . . . The feudal regime which had oppressed the people for centuries was demolished at

a stroke and in an instant. The National Assembly achieved more for the people in a few hours than the wisest and most enlightened nations had done for many centuries.[76]

The assembly did not stop at the abolishment of feudalism in France. They worked long, hard hours hammering out the foundations of the new French government. Of special importance to the legislators were the details of the relationship between that new government and the king. They had no intention at this time of doing away with the monarch—only the absolute power that he had wielded for so long.

Under the new government, the king was to share control with the legislative and judicial branches. He could no longer dictate laws

Women prepare to march on Versailles to demand bread. Among the women were men disguised as women.

that would go unchallenged; only by agreement of the other branches could laws be made. Likewise, the king's approval was necessary for the assembly's actions to become law.

Louis's reaction to the assembly's work was predictably indignant. He knew better, however, than to come right out and say that he would refuse to cooperate with the assembly. He know how vocal and powerful a mob the common people could be, and how supportive they were of the National Assembly. Better, he thought, to assure the assembly that he agreed with the *spirit* of their ideas, but that he needed time to sort out the particulars. And while he dug in his royal heels in Versailles, the mood in Paris and the countryside grew uglier.

A Stupid Mistake

The annoyance people felt with the king's stalling turned to anxiety late in September of 1789. Word leaked out that Louis had summoned another detachment of foreign soldiers—this time from Flanders. The rumors flew fast and thick. "In Paris the people pricked up their ears," writes one expert. "Weren't there enough guards at the palace? There were one hundred Swiss of the king's personal bodyguard, as well as a whole regiment of Lafayette's new National Guard. Why more?"[77]

The real reason, which many people guessed very quickly, was that Louis intended to regain his power by armed force. The plan had exploded in his face when he tried the same thing before the storming of the Bastille, and it turned out to be just as stupid a political move this time.

While people were still debating the reason for the summoning of the regiment, newspapers broke a story on October 1 that further infuriated them. It seems that a large banquet was held to welcome the Flanders regiment, at which things occurred that were highly disrespectful to the common people and the Revolution as a whole.

It was bad enough, said witnesses later, that while so many people in France were starving the partygoers had mountains of food and a limitless supply of wine. But what made matters worse was the conduct of the nobles and their guests after a great deal of that wine had been consumed. Some even went so far as to degrade the beloved symbol of the Revolution, the cockade. Mayor Bailly reported:

> Everyone's mind became heated with the astonishing profusion of wine of all kinds. Finally, in the midst of highly indecent suggestions, someone dared to insult the national tricolor cockade and toasted the white cockade which had been displayed by, amongst others, several captains of the Versailles National Guard. . . . The central courtyard of the palace then became witness to the most scandalous disorder. Royal bodyguards and officers spewed out terrible curses against the National Assembly.[78]

Such stories enraged readers, especially when more details came out. For instance, some of the banquet guests even donned the black cockade, which was the symbol of Marie Antoinette and her brother, the emperor of Austria. And because the queen was becoming more unpopular every day, stories of the court's loyalty to her were received with bitterness by the commoners.

October Days

The commoners' anger was still raging on the morning of October 5, the cold, rainy start of

"We Used Our Butt-Ends on Them and Kicked Them"

In their book The French Revolution, *editors Georges Pernoud and Sabine Flaissier include a remembrance by a young officer of the French guards. He was in Versailles when the thousands of women (and some men) marched to demand bread from the king, and he notes how rough and intimidating they were.*

"An order came to prevent the people from invading Versailles and immediately afterwards some sixty frightful women appeared announcing with loud cries that they were looking for the King and calling on everyone to join them. Seeing these harpies, who, coming from the direction of the Palais Royal increased their numbers and their intoxication at every drinking-shop they visited and many of whom brandished bludgeons and cutlasses, I made the few men remaining with me to stand to arms. I posted them in battle order in front of the gateway of Les Feuillants and I sent a corporal with four men to drive back the rabble. The only result of this was to exasperate these females and my sort of vanguard was showered with abuse and driven back. I at once supported them with the rest of my troops, which was barring the [intersection] and charged these creatures. We used our butt-ends on them and kicked them and went so far as to prick them in the stomach and the side with our bayonets. And so we drove them back fighting as far as the hill of Saint-Roch, where they threw themselves down uttering horrid imprecations and threats against us."

another week without adequate food in Paris. As always, there was bread to be found, but at prices few people could afford. What was the use of having the National Assembly making all those proclamations, people grumbled, when the king himself treated the Revolution as a joke by allowing the court to mock the cockade? And the queen was even worse, they thought, for rumors (false, in fact) were circulating that when told that the people had no bread, Marie Antoinette replied, "Let them eat cake."

That October morning there were crowds of women at the city hall of Paris, angrily complaining about the lack of bread and the bleak winter ahead. These women were not gentle or submissive. Far from it; they were rough and strong, and as one historian writes, "They were dirty and sluttish in their tattered dresses and skirts; on the whole, an ill-mannered, foul-mouthed, and vicious lot."[79]

So aggressive were they that when some suggested taking their complaints directly to the king in Versailles, the idea was met with shouts of approval. Some in the crowd also had another idea—to bring King Louis back to Paris, where he could be kept more closely informed about the plight of his subjects. Most likely, they assumed, in Versailles the king was under the influence of nobles and aristocrats who had no interest in the common people. "If only the king were in Paris, surrounded by his loving people," writes one historian, "he would accept the Revolution wholeheartedly and see to it that the city was fed properly."[80]

Through the rain, which was coming down in sheets, the crowd marched towards Versailles. Most were women, although there were men disguised as women in the crowd, too. Says Banfield, "Under those peasant bonnets poked faces covered with a most unusual stubby growth."[81] As they marched they chanted "Bread! Bread!" and shouted insults about the queen.

The mob of one thousand swelled to more than six thousand as marchers called for women to join them along the way. When some objected, saying that the weather was too rainy for such a walk, or that they had other plans, the mob threatened to cut these women's hair off unless they joined the march. The threats were believable, too, since the women were brandishing stolen weapons—even a cannon!

The King Listens

When the first wave of marchers finally reached Versailles, they were told at the palace that the king was hunting. The women went to the meeting of the National Assembly instead, and asked for bread. The stunned legislators had no choice but to listen patiently while the women demanded that the king return with them to Paris, and that those nobles who had insulted the cockade a few days before be punished swiftly.

As the members of the National Assembly listened, a second wave of demonstrators from Paris arrived. This group was even more surly and violent than the first, and carried sharp pikes, iron bars, pitchforks, and scythes. They were accompanied by Lafayette and twenty thousand members of the National Guard, who were there to ensure His Majesty's safe journey to Paris, and to make certain that things did not get out of control in Versailles.

When the king at last returned from his hunting, exhausted and muddy, he was hurriedly informed of the situation. He agreed to meet with a delegation of ten of the women from Paris. To these women, a witness wrote, "the king answered that he loved his good city of Paris too much ever to want it to lack for anything; that as long as he had been in charge of its provisioning, he thought he had done well . . . but that he would give orders and consult with the Assembly so that, the very next day, as much would be done for them as possible."[82]

The women were charmed and awed by the presence of the king, and hurried out to tell the waiting crowds that Louis had promised them assistance in getting food to Paris. But the crowd was in an angry mood. They had stood for hours in the mud and rain, and many of them were spoiling for a fight. "As soon as they came out to tell the others . . . there were shouts that it was not true," wrote one man who was there, "that they surely had been bought off."[83] Many in the crowd even called for the ten women to be hanged as enemies of the Revolution, until a deputy of the National Assembly verified the women's story.

"To Paris! To Paris!"

Early the next morning the crowd became ugly. Although the king's bodyguards wanted permission to fire on the thousands of people milling outside, Louis wanted no part of an attack on civilians. "The king," reported his children's governess, "could not accept a plan to spill his subjects' blood."[84]

Unfortunately, the crowd was not as peace loving. Even after the king's assurances that he would do whatever he could to help with the shortage of bread, the thousands of

Parisians kept up their angry chanting. The queen and her friends, not the king, were the objects of the insults; "that Austrian bitch and her playmates," as they were called scornfully.

As one witness wrote in his journals: "The palace of Versailles was in a state of turmoil all night. The queen was threatened, and people were heard to say, 'The only problem is how to share out pieces of the queen.' There was open talk of hanging her."[85]

During the night a group of demonstrators found an unlocked door in the palace and ran to Marie Antoinette's bedroom. As they noisily worked at breaking down the door, the queen jumped out of bed and took refuge in the king's room.

The violence stopped, but only after two of the royal bodyguards had been killed, and fourteen palace soldiers wounded. As the mob outside the palace chanted "To Paris! To Paris!" the king and his family stepped out onto the balcony. It was clear to the king's advisers that the crowd would not be satisfied unless Louis accompanied them back to Paris. Realizing he had little choice, Louis spoke to the crowd. "My children, you want me to follow you back to Paris: all right, I will, but on condition that I will not be separated from my wife and children."[86]

The procession back to Paris seemed endless. In addition to the royal carriage, there were fifty carts loaded with flour seized from the royal storehouses, twenty thousand National Guardsmen, and a crowd of nearly forty thousand more. Many of the women walked along next to the royal carriage, drinking and cursing the queen. As they passed people along the way, the mob shouted, "We shall have all the bread we want now, for

Bread rioters take over the Hall of the Constitution, carrying the heads of murdered guards on pikes.

we've brought the baker, the baker's wife, and the baker's boy! [the next-in-line to the throne, Louis's son]."[87]

It was an odd scene, with soldiers carrying spears upon which were impaled loaves of bread; next to them were two members of the National Guard bearing the bloody heads of the slain bodyguards on sharp pikes. In the midst of the deliriously happy crowd, the king and his family rode in silence, more like prisoners than monarchs. They would never see Versailles again.

CHAPTER 6

"There Is No Longer a King in France"

France—especially Paris—was a surprisingly peaceful place after the turmoil of the October Days. The hostility and frustration people had felt then seemed to have been replaced by devotion and happiness, even toward the queen. Writes one expert:

> The angry, menacing mobs of October 5 and 6 had, within twenty-four hours, become loving subjects. Milling around the Tuileries [the old palace in Paris that was the royal family's new home] the people kept calling for members of the royal family and cheering them. One group of women asked Marie Antoinette for the flowers and ribbons in her hair as souvenirs; graciously she gave them.[88]

Reasons for Satisfaction

There were a number of reasons for the general satisfaction people were feeling. Most important, surely, was the fact that the year's harvest was in, and had been much more bountiful than had been expected. People were more relaxed, for they knew that there would be bread at the markets; no more standing for hours in line only to be told that the shop had run out.

People were also satisfied because they felt empowered. Just look at what they had

Marie Antoinette gives alms to the poor. After the turbulent October Days, the people were more content, even to the point of forgiving Marie Antoinette.

accomplished with their unity of purpose and strength: They had marched to Versailles to get the king—and he had actually come with them! The working class had gone head to head with a centuries-old system of wealth and power, and had won.

Hadn't they demolished the ancient prison, the Bastille? The Bastille was no more than a foundation now, since it had been hauled away, brick by brick. The Parisians had made sure that the prison had not been forgotten, however, turning its demise into legend. As historian Clifford Alderman writes: "Trade was brisk at shops which sold little models of [the Bastille]. Ladies wore hats shaped like the Bastille. There was Bastille jewelry, and one could buy chips of stone guaranteed to have come from the ruins. The Theatre-Francais was sold out every night for performances of a ballet called *The Taking of the Bastille*." [89]

Changes in the Assembly

The National Assembly had followed the king to Versailles; it made far more sense for the legislators to be close to the king since they would be working together. Interestingly, however, there were many more changes in the assembly after the king's forced return to Paris.

The members of the assembly had seen the kind of raw power and violence that the mobs of common people were capable of. Many of the legislators, especially nobles and high church officials, who had joined the Third Estate in order to remain in power, were worried. If the people, when dissatisfied, could summarily murder royal bodyguards or a deputy of the Bastille prison, might that just as suddenly happen to them? Would their heads be the next on the sharp pikes of the National Guardsmen?

It was no real surprise, then, that about one-third of the members of the assembly left, either to reside far from Paris on their country estates, or to join other émigrés in nearby Germany or Belgium. Those who stayed tended to be middle-class men, members of the Third Estate. They also tended to be conservative: loyal to the king, but at the same time unwilling to compromise the progress they had made in the Revolution thus far.

The constitution which this assembly drafted exemplified their political thinking. It called for a division of power between the king and the assembly, a system of checks and balances similar to the one in the United States. According to this new constitution, there would be no more censorship over what was written in France. Full freedom

The Declaration of the Rights of Man and the Citizen ended the ancien régime and granted rights to the common people of France.

of speech was guaranteed. There would be open trials from now on, quite unlike the old system whereby a person could be thrown in prison at the whim of a king or other high official.

Members of the Third Estate were granted more privileges than ever before in this constitution—but not all members of the Third Estate. For example, only people with specified amounts of property or wealth could vote, and it followed that these professional and working people would elect people like themselves as legislators. The peasants and the urban poor, though a factor in the Revolution, were not a key part of this new government.

New Thinking on the Church

One aspect of the ancien régime that had not gone away was the financial crisis. Years of spending and borrowing had left France's treasuries almost empty, and the assembly had not done anything to fill them. Not surprisingly, the legislators were reluctant to levy new taxes or increase existing ones for fear of alienating the common people.

But without money, the government would collapse; the members of the assembly knew that. So when one legislator reminded the others of an untapped source of great wealth in France, there was immediate enthusiasm. That source was the enormous land holdings of the church—more than 25 percent of the wealth of France. Peasants and wealthy merchants were eager to buy whatever land they could afford. By putting these parcels of land on the auctioneer's block, the government was able to raise a fortune.

However, intervention by the government into church affairs did not stop there.

Lawmakers decided to do something about problems they had been aware of for many years, such as the luxurious lifestyles of some who lived in convents and monasteries. "For years writers had poked fun at the decadence of monks and nuns," explains one historian, "painting scathing portraits of the rich men and women who led genteel, sheltered lives in buildings that looked more like chateaux [country mansions] than homes for those who had taken vows of poverty."[90] Very soon the government called for the abolishment of such places.

The state exercised more and more control over church hierarchy, dictating new terms under which bishops and other church employees were hired. No longer were they chosen by the aristocracy, nor could wealthy nobles purchase high positions in the church. Bishops would be elected by the same rules by which other government officials were elected. High clergy found its salaries lowered far below previous levels, and the lowly, hard-working parish priests were paid twice as much as before.

A Very Controversial Move

The most controversial of the government's church reforms concerned an oath that the assembly demanded all priests and clergymen take. Every employee of the church would be required to swear to be loyal to the Revolution, and to the government of France with its new constitution.

This was a new role for the church, one that differed fundamentally from the traditionally independent one enjoyed for centuries. Instead, says one historian, "it [was to be] the servant of the state, a sort of moral agent whose job was to make people into better citizens."[91]

Although legislators in the new government assumed full authority over the church, the true head of all French Catholics was the pope, and he did not approve of the government's involvement. From Rome, Pope Pius VI made his objections very clear to high officials in France: God directed the affairs of the church, the pope warned, not legislators. The government was not God.

Out of loyalty to the pope, many priests and other officials announced their refusal to take the oath to the government, and heated controversy ensued. The day scheduled for all priests to take the oath was January 16, 1791, and people throughout France waited anxiously to see what would happen.

"It is not hard to imagine the tension of the people who flocked to Mass on that cold January morning," comments historian Sarel Eimerl.

> In Paris the priests were especially unpopular, and the city seethed with excitement. Afraid fights would break out, the city government had ordered out the National Guard and everywhere the streets were lined with soldiers. Inside the churches, the congregations waited impatiently for the priests to announce their decisions.[92]

The decisions, as it turned out, were split quite evenly. Many priests took the oath, perhaps intimidated by their revolution-minded congregations. Others refused and were booed lustily by the crowds that filled the churches. In many churches, government officials fired the priests on the spot for treason, which is what happened at the Church of Saint Sulpice near Paris.

"Citizens!" shouted the government official who took the pulpit there immediately after the priest announced his refusal to swear the oath. "By his refusal to swear allegiance to the nation, this man has incurred dismissal from the public employment which was entrusted to him. He will soon no longer be your pastor and you will be called upon to name another more worthy of your confidence."[93]

Deciding to Flee

It was, say historians, a huge mistake for the legislators and leaders of the Revolution to require such an oath of loyalty, for it forced people to choose between two things that they dearly valued, the Revolution and their religion. The large number of priests who refused the oath found surprising support from their congregations. "Thousands of the nation's faithful," writes one expert, "loyal to the men who had married them, baptized their children, and buried their dead, followed these priests' lead and protested the reforms."[94]

One man who disagreed wholeheartedly with the new government's ecclesiastical reforms was His Majesty King Louis XVI. Up until the assembly's interference with the church, the king had tried to keep a low profile. He certainly disagreed with all manner of various reforms, but he was not in a position to fight the assembly, at least not openly. The queen, on the other hand, was very vocal about her feelings. She was furious at the way the government had stripped the monarchy of power.

The queen felt humiliated by her family's forced move to Paris, too. Accustomed to the spacious, airy rooms at Versailles, she felt imprisoned in the dark, gloomy Tuileries. She and her children had been given suites of rooms on the ground floor, where people wanting to gawk at the royal family could literally press against the outside windows and look in at all hours of the day or night.

The queen wanted Louis to regain his former status, and was quite definite about how she wanted her husband to fight the Revolution. "[She] wanted him to go to Austria, raise an army, and return to wipe out the revolutionaries," writes one historian, "but the king, in his fuzzy way, was fond of his subjects and could not bring himself to agree."[95]

Moreover, Louis was reluctant to ask for outside help. He knew that many émigrés would be more than willing to raise armies and help attack the revolutionary government of France—for a price. The king did not want to risk having the outsiders seize power themselves when they returned. So when secret messages came to him from émigrés willing to help him escape, or to send troops to France to fight the government, he ignored them.

Louis XVI's elaborate plans to escape from Paris across the border into Austria failed miserably after he was captured at Varennes. Once caught, the people became extremely hostile toward the king.

But the controversy concerning the church and the government was just the push Louis needed. He was a devout Catholic who could not bear to see the church compromised by oaths to the Revolution. Now, when Marie Antoinette and the émigrés proposed schemes for his escape from France, he was willing to consider them.

Royal Runaways

Finally, a plan was devised for Louis and his family to flee the Tuileries and head northeast to the border of France and the Austrian Netherlands. There a general loyal to the king would meet them and guide them over the border. Soon afterwards, it was hoped, the revolutionary government would be seized by outside armies friendly to Louis, and he would return to the throne.

A handful of people at the palace in Paris helped the royal family climb into a carriage on the night of June 20, 1791. Although the escape went as planned at the beginning of the journey, Louis was recognized 124 miles from Paris by a village postmaster. In the little town of Varennes, the family was arrested and held until the National Guard could come to escort its members back to Paris.

If the crowds were unfriendly during the October Days in Versailles, they were murderously hostile towards the king and queen as they rode back to Paris. More than 150,000 people accompanied the royal family home, and a great deal of effort by the National Guard ensured that the king and queen were publicly humiliated on the trip. A long, roundabout route was chosen, so that as many people as possible could view the royal carriage. The flight to Varennes had taken but a day; it took four full days to return to Paris.

"Hat on Your Head"

All along the route, the crowds jeered and shouted profanities into the open windows of the carriage (the National Guard had ordered the doors and windows opened so people could get a good look inside). "Fat pig" and "ugly traitor" were frequently used insults hurled at the king, while Marie Antoinette was scorned and mocked with unprintable names. One witness wrote that "the young prince . . . began to shriek in terror; the Queen held him on her lap, tears were falling from her eyes."[96]

One Paris newspaper described the crowd's reaction to the return of the king. "Women competed with men over the guard of the city gates, telling them, 'It was women who brought the King to Paris, it was men who let him escape.' But the men replied, 'Ladies, do not boast so much, that was no great prize you brought us.'"[97]

But as the procession entered the city, the atmosphere changed dramatically. The people there had been instructed by the National Guard and other leaders to wear their hats, a sign of disrespect since people normally removed their hats to the king. One visitor to Paris from England recalls, "An officer passed us about half an hour before the King's arrival and called out as he passed: 'Chapeau sur tete' ['Hat on your head']. This order was punctually observed."[98]

So instead of being unruly and riotous, the Paris crowds were silent and staring. The National Guard stood at attention along the streets, as was the custom in funeral processions, with muskets reversed. Drummers beat a slow, steady death march. As one historian writes, "The silence as the carriage entered

A Plan That Almost Worked

In his book Voices of the French Revolution, *editor Richard Cobb includes a diary entry by the marquis de Bouille, a friend of the king. In this entry, the marquis discusses the arrangements Louis had made for the flight from Paris—an escape that ended in the king's imprisonment.*

"On 27 May the king wrote to me that he would leave on 19 June, between midnight and one o'clock; that he would go in an ordinary carriage as far as Bondy, one post stage from Paris, and there take his own carriage which should be awaiting him. One of his bodyguards, appointed to act as courier, should wait there in case the king did not arrive by two o'clock, which would show that he had been unable to leave. This same bodyguard should go straight to Pont-de Sommevelle to bring me news so that I might look to my own safety.

The king also said that if he were not recognized along the route, and if there were no disturbance amongst the people, then he would travel incognito and would not make use of the escort, which would follow some hours behind. The day after I received this letter from the king, I instructed [an associate] to order his men to be at Varennes on 19 June, with horses ready to serve as relays for the king's carriage."

Marie Antoinette endured murderously hostile crowds upon her return with the king from their failed escape to Varennes. Witnesses claimed the humiliating event caused the queen's blond hair to turn completely gray during the four-day procession back to Paris.

Paris and slowly drove through its streets was complete: instead of the usual bustle, the noise of traffic, the cries of the street vendors, all now was quietly menacing."[99]

For the king and queen, this reception was even harder to bear than the insults along the way. Louis was overheard to murmur, "There is no longer a King in France."[100] And the stress and shame took their toll on Marie Antoinette: Witnesses said that when the thirty-five-year-old queen stepped out of her carriage, her ash blond hair had, during the four-day journey, turned completely gray, like that of an old woman.

The Sansculottes

Interestingly, while the lower classes of French society watched in grim, angry silence as the king and queen were returned to the Tuileries, most of the members of the National Assembly were more than willing to forgive the king for his escape attempt. After all, they had been working hard on the constitution for the new government, and that constitution clearly specified that power was to be shared between an assembly and the king. "[The assembly] really had no choice," writes one expert. "If a constitutional monarchy was to be maintained, it would need a King, and the one now imprisoned in his Palace was the only one readily available."[101]

The alternative—getting rid of the king and forming a republic—was not at all attractive to the members of the assembly. The majority of them were bourgeois men leading comfortable lives. They worried that a republic, a government based solely on the will of the majority of the people, would endanger the progress they'd made in the Revolution by giving more power to the lower classes.

Their fears were well founded. There was a great deal of unrest among the poor people of Paris, for they were the only segment of the Third Estate who had not seen their lives improve since the Revolution. Even the rural peasants had benefited by the abolition of feudal dues and responsibilities.

The urban lower class's lack of progress was certainly not from lack of participation. On the contrary, the people of Paris felt that they had done most of the hard work of the Revolution, with no rewards. As historian Eimerl comments, "They had stormed the Bastille. They had marched on Versailles and brought the King back to Paris. They had formed the National Guard, the citizen army that had scared the King off from sending in his own soldiers to retake control of Paris." [102]

If anything, these people were in a worse situation now than before, for rampant unemployment and high prices made their lives increasingly more difficult. "These poor Parisians felt they had been betrayed," Eimerl writes. "They had driven the King and his noble friends from power. Now the bourgeois had taken control of the government and they seemed to be just as selfish as the nobles." [103]

The urban working class had begun calling themselves by a new name—*sansculottes*, which means "without knee breeches." The nobles had traditionally worn silk pants fitted just below the knee; common men wore long trousers. For the urban poor, their baggy trousers had become as much a badge of the Revolution as the red, white, and blue cockade. Now the sansculottes were on the rise, the forgotten people of the Revolution, but determined to be heard.

The Rise of Political Clubs

One measure of the sansculottes' increased involvement was the rise of various political clubs. Once reserved for the more well-to-do members of society, clubs were springing up all over the city, giving working people the opportunity to share their views on the government. Eimerl describes the typical gathering:

> Some of the sansculottes might be wearing the red cap of the Revolution, a woolen cap with an end piece which hung down behind like a pony tail. . . . The air was dense with tobacco smoke. Glasses of rough, red wine stood on the tables. Amid the noise and the smoke, the sansculottes listened to the words of their leaders stirring them up to take action against their new masters—the bourgeois. [104]

Some of these clubs were more conservative than others. The Jacobins, which had been around for several years, tended to be less radical in their beliefs. They had hundreds of chapters throughout France, and

During the French Revolution, many small political clubs formed to discuss ideas. One was the conservative Jacobins, who met in this building.

were highly influential in provincial governments, for they gave people a way to express their views at the local level.

The Cordelier Club favored more radical methods to gain political clout for the masses, and the sansculottes seemed to be flocking to them in greater and greater numbers. For one thing, their membership dues were a small fraction of the fees charged by the Jacobins. The Cordeliers talked frequently of removing the king from power and forming a republic, taking control away from the bourgeoisie and assuming it for themselves. After the king's attempted escape, a physician and Cordelier activist named Jean-Paul Marat published this scathing attack in a radical Paris newspaper:

> Who can be so blind as not to see that the King, who not only fled but denounced the constitution . . . has thus forfeited all right to the crown. If the Assembly were not the accomplice of Louis XVI's treason, it would have deposed him. . . . The indignant nation . . . declares Louis XVI unfit to reign. . . . The wife of the ex-monarch, that ferocious mover of the court's crimes, must be shorn and jailed. . . . [Louis] has been brought back within our walls, this crowned brigand, perjurer, traitor, and conspirator . . . as cowardly as he is stupid.[105]

Massacre on the Champ de Mars

The Cordeliers' charges that the assembly was an accomplice to the king seemed close to the truth when on July 15, 1791, the legislators voted the king innocent of any wrongdoing. The only stipulation to their ruling was that Louis must accept the new constitution.

The news enraged the sansculottes, who immediately set to work planning a fitting response to the assembly's actions. The Cordeliers hastily circulated petitions that called for the end of the monarchy and for Louis to be put on trial for treason. In addition, they called for a mass demonstration at the Champ de Mars, a large parade ground on the west side of the city.

On Sunday, July 17, a crowd of fifty thousand gathered in opposition to the assembly's decision. Violence erupted and the National Guard was called in to disperse the throngs of people. The National Guard, led by Lafayette, carried a red flag, the signal that martial law was being imposed.

The crowd grew more angry and pelted the soldiers with stones. One witness claimed that the Guard fired on the crowd without waiting for a command, for they were hot and tired and irritated that they had to spend their Sunday afternoon in this way:

> [The mob] began . . . to pelt [the soldiers] with stones. It was hot weather and it was Sunday afternoon, for which time, according to usage immemorial, the inhabitants of this capital have generally some pleasurable engagement. To be disappointed in their amusement, to be paraded through streets through a scorching sun, and then stand, like holiday turkeys, to be knocked down by brickbats was a little more than they had patience to bear; so that, without waiting for orders, they fired.[106]

When the shooting was over, fifty demonstrators lay dead or dying and the crowd was dispersed, but the assembly decided to punish the Cordeliers and other sansculottes further. They quickly passed laws abolishing the Cordeliers clubs, and forbade the publishing of all newspapers critical of the king

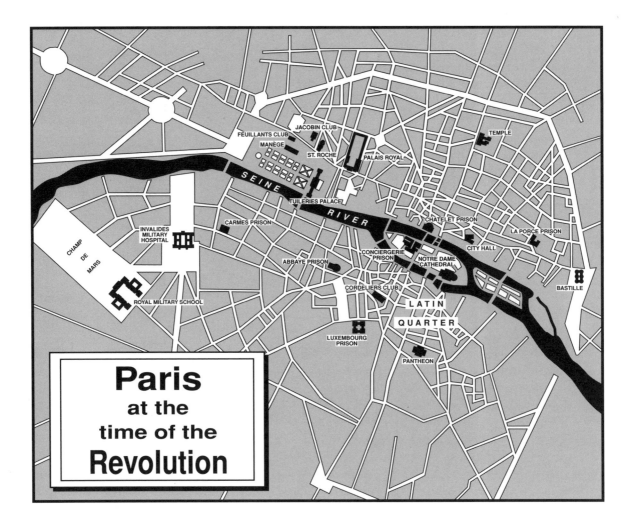

Paris at the time of the Revolution

or the assembly. Arrest warrants were issued for radical leaders. The freedoms of speech and of the press that had been proclaimed by the assembly and the new constitution were for the time shelved.

It might have seemed to some in France that order had been restored. The king had agreed to the terms of the assembly, agreeing to abide by the constitution so that he could be restored to power. But although the sansculottes had been silenced and their presses shut down, many unresolved issues remained. Although things seemed peaceful and calm, the fury of the masses seethed just below the surface. The poor people of France would not be silent for long.

France on the March

One effect of the massacre at the Champ de Mars on French politics could be seen that autumn, in the elections of 1791. With the drafting and signing of the constitution, the National Assembly's work was complete. The task of governing France was to be shared by the king and a new elected body, the Legislative Assembly. As voters learned, the deputies elected to the new body were of a different political stripe than their predecessors.

"A Mass of Villains, of Madmen, and of Idiots"

There were no urban poor or peasants elected to the assembly—none of those classes were even allowed to vote. Those who did vote were generally wealthy, middle-class bourgeois—and they tended to elect men like themselves. However, some of the views these new deputies held were far from conservative.

There were no monarchists among the deputies elected to the Legislative Assembly, no men whose primary loyalty was to the king. In their place were a great many new deputies who were quite liberal—even radical—and loyal to the sansculottes. Of these deputies, comments one historian, "all were hostile to the King, all demanded radical change, and most were willing to work together with the Paris mob, whom they often harangued and with whom they met at the clubs."[107]

To the king and queen, this new assembly's hostility to the throne was a worry. Said Marie Antoinette of the new deputies, "There is nothing to be done with this Assembly: it is a mass of villains, of madmen, and of idiots."[108]

The Girondins

Many of the new deputies came from an area in southern France along the Atlantic coast called Gironde. These deputies, known as the Girondins, had been very active in the Jacobin clubs, and tended to be young, liberal, and very outspoken about their revolutionary ideas. They had quite a lot of influence in the assembly and immediately set to work introducing legislation tailored to their particular politics.

The presence of so many priests who refused to take the oath of loyalty, for instance, was a constant source of conflict and divisiveness in France. The Girondins wanted those priests to take the oath once and for all, or be imprisoned as enemies of the Revolution.

The émigrés, too, were considered a threat to France. They sat in comfort far from Paris, in foreign countries, where they urged foreign monarchs to help restore Louis to the throne. Because they were a potential threat to the Revolution, many leaders in France wanted the émigrés to be forced to return to France, where they could be controlled. The Girondins and other like-minded

Émigrés on the March

Although many of the French nobles and their families had fled France, fearing for their lives, a good number of them had not given up on the monarchy. These émigrés, such as the marquis de Faliaiseau, who wrote the following letter to his wife in 1792, were aiding some of the foreign armies who were fighting against the armies of the Revolution.

"Since Monday evening, dearest, we have been in France. We had a long and tiring march and are now about two and a half leagues from Thionville. The village in which we are now is fairly large. The inhabitants are very 'patriotic.'. . . .

Up to now Thionville has not surrendered and it appears that the citizens mean to defend it. We are bringing up guns for the siege. In the first village through which we passed, the people cried, 'Long live the King,' to which we replied with a lusty cheer.

The former parish-priests have been reinstated. Just now some [police] brought along a 'constitutional priest' [one who had taken the oath] bound and gagged—a great rascal, they say. I spoke to the man, who claimed to have taken the oath conscientiously, because the King had sanctioned the civil constitution. . . .

If we are successful, as appears likely, nothing can stop us marching on Paris and arriving there soon. . . . The King of Prussia has issued a communication to the inhabitants of France containing a warning to the city of Paris to the effect that the Town can still escape destruction, if the good citizens will liberate the King . . . but that if the King loses his life the innocent will suffer with the guilty, when the town is sacked. . . .

Adieu. The trumpet sounds and we must get ready to resume our march."

deputies drafted new laws calling for all émigrés to return or face death sentences.

Frustration—and an Answer

However, it is one thing to draft legislation, and quite another to pass those measures into law. Louis's powers had been considerably diminished by the National Assembly, but he still had the power of veto, and he used it liberally and effectively. No death warrants would be issued for émigrés who refused to come back to France. No imprisonment for priests who would not take the oath.

The Girondins were frustrated. The king's lack of cooperation was tying their hands. What was equally frustrating was that old problems were resurfacing, too. Political unrest had caused more fear in the countryside; nervousness about the future made people worry about their food supply. Grain convoys en route to Paris were being attacked almost on a daily basis. And the Jacobins, who loved to use fear as a tool to stir up activity among the poor, were capitalizing on it all. Rumors everywhere warned of enemies of the Revolution plotting their revenge on the peasants who had benefited from the new reforms.

The Girondin's explanation as to why nothing was being accomplished in their Legislative Assembly—and why things seemed to have gotten worse since they were elected—was that no one would cooperate with them. "They were telling people what to do but nobody would listen," writes Sarel Eimerl. "The farmers wouldn't bring their food to the towns. Priests wouldn't take the oath. The King wouldn't sign their decrees. The Jacobins wouldn't keep quiet."[109] What France lacked were programs that everyone—not just one group or another—could support wholeheartedly.

There seemed to be one idea, however, that did not fragment society, one that was appealing to just about everyone: war. For months many radicals in Paris had suggested this course—declare war on the nations surrounding France, those who were harboring and supporting the hated émigrés. One Girondin leader, Jacques-Pierre Brissot, proposed declaring war as a way of uniting the nation. "War is actually a national benefit," Brissot explained. "A people . . . needs war to purge away the vices of despotism, it needs war to banish from its bosom the men who might corrupt liberty."[110]

Radicals throughout France hailed the idea as a good one, and even expanded on its goals. Not only could such a war strike out at the enemies of France, but it would also bring the Revolution to other lands where people were oppressed by tyrants like Louis XVI.

Surprisingly, the idea of war had strong support from Louis himself, although for far different reasons. He had been secretly corresponding with monarchs in other lands, as well as with some émigrés, and he had no doubt that the untested National Guard of France would be easily defeated. When that happened, reasoned the king, it would be easy for foreign forces to take over the gov-

ernment in Paris, and Louis would regain his throne. In a letter to her brother, Emperor Leopold of Austria, Marie Antoinette wrote, "Everything has been overturned by force and force alone can repair the damage."[111]

Publicly, however, Louis supported the idea of war as a way to unite the French people. On April 20, 1792, he spoke to the Legislative Assembly and urged them to declare war. "All would rather have war," he stated, "than see the dignity of the French people insulted any longer. I have now come to propose war."[112]

"All We Need Is Whips"

The agreed-upon enemy in the proposed war was to be Austria. It was the birthplace of the hated queen, a land that her brother now ruled. Austria, an enemy of France for many years, had been supportive of émigrés who lived within her borders. Altogether, it was a logical choice.

The news that their country was going to war seemed to lift the spirits of the French people. Optimism reigned, as in a letter a Girondin deputy wrote on April 21: "I have no doubt that the zeal of the French, their honour and patriotism, the entirely justifiable enticements which will be used to open the eyes of the foreign soldiers at long last, and the general anxiety of the peoples—all these will lead to victory for us on the frontier."[113]

His assessment was wholly inaccurate, however. From the outset, the war was a disaster for France. The National Guard was unprepared for combat, and most of the French troops threw down their weapons and ran at the first sight of an Austrian soldier. One French general whose officers suspected him of treason was seized by his own men and hanged. The Austrians were bemused by the cowardice and disorganization of the French soldiers. "We do not need swords to put the French to flight," one Austrian soldier snorted. "All we need is whips." [114]

France's poor performance in the opening battles of the war had dire effects throughout the country. The economy, which was already shaky, took a sudden downward turn. Food shortages and runaway inflation plagued the people of France, and they turned their anger toward the Girondins, who, say historians, "were thunderstruck; defeat had never entered into their schemes." [115] Their response was to deflect the anger of the people towards Louis.

"The Throne Still Stood, but the People Had Sat on It"

It seemed just a matter of time until the crowds of angry people milling around the streets of Paris stormed the Tuileries. They had heard enough from the king and the Legislative Assembly to realize that nothing was being accomplished. Whatever measures the assembly did manage to pass were quickly vetoed by the king. The Revolution appeared at a standstill, and the people had had enough of the stalling.

On the morning of June 20, 1792, a mob of more than eight thousand burst into the room where the assembly was meeting, and then charged into the Tuileries. Chanting "No veto! No veto!" they rampaged through the palace, dragging a cannon up the stairs, and attacked various locked doors with axes and hammers. One man carried a calf's heart, still dripping blood, which was labeled "The heart of an aristocrat."

Part of the mob located the queen and her children and chased them into the Council Room. The palace guard tried their best to protect the royal family, who cringed nervously behind a massive oak and

Hordes of angry citizens enter the Palace of the Tuileries. The king's nine hundred Swiss guards were unable to fend off their attack.

ivory table while the crowd called Marie Antoinette "slut" and "dog." At last rioters burst into the king's stateroom, loudly demanding that he stop vetoing the assembly's reforms. The king, say historians, was uncharacteristically courageous and calm in the face of the hostile mob. He told them that he would not be swayed from doing what he thought was right—especially not by threats. "Force will have no effect on me," he declared. "I cannot be terrorized."[116]

Someone in the crowd thrust a *bonnet rouge*, the red woolen cap and badge of liberty, onto the king's head. Another handed him a bottle of wine, and His Majesty drank a toast to the people's health. He would not, however, change his mind about the vetoes. Then, after a few hours of milling around inside the palace, the steam having gone out of their demonstration, the crowd dispersed.

Interpretations of the event varied according to individual perspectives. Louis, on the one hand, believed that his brave demeanor in the face of danger had taught the unruly mob a lesson, and that the French people would respect him for it:

> The French will not have learned without sorrow that an armed multitude led into error by a few factious men broke into the King's residence, pulled cannon as far as the Guard Hall, broke down the doors of his apartment with axes, and there abusively claiming to be the nation, tried to obtain by force the consent that His Majesty constitutionally refused to two decrees. The King met the menaces and the insults of these factious men with no force other than his conscience and his love of the public welfare. . . .
>
> If those who want to end the monarchy need yet another crime, they may

Sansculottes threaten and humiliate King Louis XVI, forcing him to wear the red cap of a revolutionary.

commit it. In its current state of crisis, the King will give to the last moment . . . an example of the courage and firmness that alone can save France.[117]

There was another view, however—one held by some of the most radical revolutionaries in Paris. Jean-Paul Marat, who had begun publishing his hard-hitting editorials once again, saw the end of the monarchy in the people's invasion of the Tuileries. "The events of the twentieth of June," he wrote, "dissipated the prestige of the inviolability of the Palace, of the King's person, and of the monarchy. The throne still stood, but the people had sat on it and had taken its measure."[118]

Marat's assessment was eerily foreboding. The people would invade the king's palace again very soon, and the next time the mob would not leave empty-handed. There were not enough soldiers in the king's guard to fight the enemy that would come then.

"The Day of Glory Now Is Here!"

While the political climate of Paris became more and more heated, the war effort continued to sour. To make matters worse, news reached Paris that the leader of the Austrian forces had issued a proclamation to the revolutionaries of France: If the royal family were harmed in any way, the foreign armies would level Paris, sparing no one.

The Austrian leader's edict caused a panic in Paris. What would happen if the powerful enemy marched into their city, intent on slaughter? What would become of them? A plea was sent to all the districts of France—volunteers were needed to protect the city, to save it from being overrun. France responded.

The most notable of the volunteers came from Marseilles, far south of Paris. As they marched they sang a stirring, patriotic song, which captured the hearts of the French people. They referred to it as "The Marseillaise Hymn"—and it would one day become the national anthem of France:

> Come children of the fatherland,
> The day of glory now is here!
> To arms citizens!
> Form your battalions!
> March on! March on![119]

One newspaper reported that the song was so popular in Paris that it was sung at weddings, at funerals, and even between acts at plays throughout the city. "In all our houses of entertainment the public always calls for the song. . . . The tune is both moving and martial. [The soldiers] sing it with the greatest fervor and the passage where, waving their hats and brandishing their swords, they all sing together, *Aux armes, citoyens* ['To arms, citizens'] is truly thrilling."[120]

"Kill One in Every Ten"

The men from Marseilles and other National Guardsmen from districts of France more remote from Paris were not only willing to risk their lives defending their country from foreign invaders, they were also avid revolutionaries. Historians say that, with some urging from the Jacobins and the Cordeliers, these troops were spoiling for a fight—and the king and his deputies seemed to be a more readily available target than the Austrians, at least for the moment.

One citizen of Paris at that time recalled how violent and wild the atmosphere in the city became after the arrival of "these beastly [soldiers] spewed up by Marseilles. . . . One cannot imagine anything more horrifying than these 500 fanatics, three-quarters of them drunk, almost all wearing red bonnets, marching bare-armed and disheveled. . . . They fraternized at all the drinking shops with groups as dangerous as themselves."[121]

As the hot August days went by, plans to dethrone the king were debated in every café, in every bar. People were not secretive or careful about such talk—it was all very open. They were urged on by the writings of Jean-Paul Marat, who reminded the people of Paris that they should strike first at the government, since they would certainly be killed by the counterrevolutionaries, the armies of those who were friends of the king and the émigrés. He wrote:

> Fear the reaction; your enemies will not spare you. You are lost forever if you do not lop off the rotten branches at the [local government levels]. . . . I therefore propose that you kill one in every ten of the counterrevolutionary members of the municipality, the courts . . . and the Assembly. . . . Hold the King, his wife, and his son as hostages until they can be tried, let him be shown four times every day to the people. . . . Warn him that if, within two weeks, the Austrians and the Prussians are closer than twenty leagues [about 50 miles] to our borders . . . he will lose his head.[122]

"All Paris Is Marching"

It seemed throughout the day of August 9 that there could not be more tension in the city; the very air seemed electric with it. It was another hot, sultry day, and menacing crowds milled around the palace. Someone on horseback was trying to pull down a statue of Louis XIV on the lawn; others were shouting threats and insults past the windows. The king's guard, which consisted of some still-loyal members of the National Guard as well as paid Swiss soldiers, watched the movements of the crowd nervously.

The night passed fitfully; at 1:00 A.M. church bells throughout the city began clanging. Hour after hour they sounded, and although there seemed to be no movement at first, by dawn it was clear that the people of France were on the march. Radical leaders forcibly occupied the city government and

Mobs storm the Palace at Tuileries, carrying whatever weapons they can manage.

announced a new revolutionary government, called a Commune, had taken its place. And thousands upon thousands of armed citizens, "who had been waiting in doorways all night, were joining into a vast mass and marching, marching, marching," writes one historian. "The sound of their voices raised in song could . . . be heard in the distance."[123]

Inside the Tuileries, loyal deputies urged the king to flee. They knew that there were not enough soldiers loyal to the king left in France to fight off the mobs that were approaching the palace. As Olivier Bernier writes, one deputy recalled telling the king and queen that their only chance of safety was to escape to the headquarters of the Legislative Assembly. The body had been meeting all night, frantically trying to prevent what now seemed inevitable. But neither Louis nor Marie Antoinette would believe that mobs were really approaching.

> The deputy answered, "Sire, there are twelve cannons and a huge crowd is coming in. . . ."
> "But, Monsieur," the Queen said, "we have defenders." "Madame," answered the deputy, "all Paris is marching."[124]

The royal family did escape, by running across the gardens to the assembly meeting hall, so they were gone when the mob broke through the doors of the Tuileries and the vicious fighting started. National Guard soldiers joined thousands of citizens armed with knives, guns, bayonets, swords, wooden clubs, and sharp pikes in their fight against the Swiss guards.

Ironically, it was the king's aversion to bloodshed that resulted in the bloody massacre of more than one thousand of the royal soldiers. Louis sent word that his Swiss guards were to cease fighting, to surrender to the crowd. The mob was not interested in taking prisoners, however. "No sooner had the defenders laid down their arms," writes one historian, "than they were overwhelmed by the maddened crowd. A few survived to be flung into prison, but most of them were slaughtered where they stood. Their bodies, horribly mutilated, were dragged out of the palace, some even as far as the square in front of the city hall, and left lying on the ground."[125]

The Changed Face of Paris

The fall of the city government meant that the Legislative Assembly was insecure as well. Its members knew, as they listened to the shouts of the mob ransacking the Tuileries and murdering the king's guards, that they dare not allow the monarchy to continue. There was no way to resist the tens of thousands of angry people demanding an end to the king's rule; the assembly voted that night to suspend Louis from his duties as king and to hold him and his family prisoner in the Temple, a fortified castle, until his future could be decided.

Historians say that the events of August 10, 1792, completely changed the face of Paris. With the city government now in the hands of the radical new Commune, the city seemed to close down. "The gates out of the city were shut," explains one expert. "Aristocrats who had not managed to escape went into hiding, and foreign countries recalled their ambassadors. The ancien régime had truly come to an end."[126]

Just what direction the new government would take would be revealed to the people of France—in the days and months ahead.

Down with the King!

With the king stripped of all power and now literally a prisoner, the government of France was temporarily in chaos. The constitution was worthless, for it had called for both a Legislative Assembly and a monarchy working together; without the monarch, the document was null and void.

Until a new constitution could be written and adopted, the assembly appointed a six-man council to rule France. Five of the six were Girondins; the sixth man, who was destined to be one of the most important figures of the Revolution, was a brassy-voiced, burly Jacobin named Georges Danton.

A Man of the People

Danton had been a leader of the Cordeliers before, a radical revolutionary who thought that the reforms and changes in the government so far had not gone far enough. A lawyer, Danton had earned a very comfortable living in that profession. But even though he had money, he disliked aristocrats and the "respectable" bourgeoisie.

His real loyalties were to the sansculottes, the poor of Paris. And they liked him, too. He was a big man, with what one historian describes as a "brutally battered prize-fighter's face," pitted with scars from acne, smallpox, and childhood accidents.[127] His voice was big and booming, and he used it to his advantage, bellowing out his opinions in the cafés and bars of Paris.

He had a well-deserved reputation for being a ladies' man, a hard drinker, and a dirty fighter, all of which makes his strong devotion to his wife seem surprising. Historians say that he enjoyed nothing more than sitting on his porch with his wife, having quiet conversations after dinner. So much did he love her, in fact, that when she died unexpectedly while he was on a trip to Belgium, "he had her dug up seven days after her

Minister of Justice Georges Danton worked hard to unite the various revolutionary contingents. Well liked by the people, he also encouraged mob violence.

death," writes one historian, "and sobbed with her crumbling body in his arms."[128]

"His principles were incendiary, his speeches violent and furious," recalled one associate, "but in private, he was easy, had the loosest morals and was utterly cynical. He loved women and despised life. He had a soul; his eloquence was volcanic; he was built altogether to be the spokesman of the people."[129]

In Georges Danton the sansculottes of Paris got a political voice almost immediately after he was picked for the council. Although the Girondins on the committee were far more moderate than he, he was able to muscle through new legislation giving all adult males the right to vote, dictating that all priests refusing to take the oath of loyalty be banished, and ordering that all property of émigrés be promptly put on the market and sold.

"Daring, More Daring, and Again Daring"

As Danton was busying himself with social and political reforms, the news from the battlefront continued to be grim. The combined armies of Prussia, Austria, and various émigré troops had moved across the northern border into France, and were anticipating a move toward Paris. The French troops were unable to mount any sort of challenge against the enemy, and an invasion of the capital seemed inevitable.

Danton's superb oratory served him well in this time of national emergency. He implored the people to be strong, to fight for the Revolution and for France. On September 2, 1792, he addressed the assembly about the need for more young men to come forward and volunteer for the army. The conclusion of this speech yielded one of the most famous quotations in French history,

as well known as Patrick Henry's "Give me liberty or give me death" speech in American history. Passionately he rallied the delegates:

> All France is roused, all France is on the move. All France is burning with the desire to fight. . . . The tocsin [warning] that we are going to sound is no alarm bell, it is the signal for the charge against the enemies of the fatherland. To vanquish them, gentlemen, we must show daring, more daring, and again daring; and France will be saved.[130]

The response to Danton's speech was overwhelming. Within days, thousands of young men streamed out of Paris, marching north to join the battle against the Prussians, the Austrians, and the émigré forces. But although the nation cheered them as they left, their departure raised other concerns for the citizens of Paris. After all, wasn't the Revolution being fought right there in the city by common people like themselves? Who would fight the battles against the nobles and the aristocrats while the men were gone to the north, fighting the foreign invaders?

The city's inhabitants were made even more anxious by rumors that the invaders were in communication with the counterrevolutionaries in the Paris prisons. If the prisoners escaped or were freed by the invaders from the north, went the rumors, they would seek revenge on the sansculottes.

"His Solutions Were Always Direct and Bloody"

No one fueled these rumors more than Jean-Paul Marat, whose angry voice predated the Revolution. He had been forced underground after the Champ de Mars massacre,

A Portrait of Marat

One of Jean-Paul Marat's contemporaries wrote a very detailed description of the colorful revolutionary leader. It is included in Elizabeth Wormeley Latimer's book My Scrap-Book of the French Revolution. *It is obvious by the description that the writer sympathizes with Marat's political views.*

Radical journalist Jean-Paul Marat played a part in encouraging the crowds to murder members of the Swiss guard and the clergy. "I believe in cutting off of heads," he once said.

"Marat was a very small man, hardly five feet high; but he was strongly built, neither too fat nor too lean. . . . He used his arms gracefully, and with much gesticulation. His neck was short, his face broad and bony. His nose was aquiline, but it looked as if it had been flattened. His mouth had a contraction at one corner. His forehead was wide, his eyes light hazel, full of spirit, life, and keenness; their natural expression was gentle and kindly. His eyebrows were scanty, his complexion sallow, his beard dark, his hair brown and disorderly.

He walked rapidly, with his head thrown back. His favorite attitude was to cross his arms over his chest. He gesticulated a great deal when he talked in company, and would stamp his foot to emphasize his words; sometimes he would rise on tiptoe when he became vehement. His voice was sonorous, but he had a defect in his tongue which made it hard for him to pronounce clearly *c* and *s*. Yet when accustomed to his voice, the earnestness of his thoughts, the plenitude of his expressions, the simplicity of his eloquence, and the brevity of his words, his hearers forgot the slight defect in his enunciation."

when the assembly had forbidden the publishing of any newspapers critical of the king or the government, but he had still continued to publish his radical newsletter from the sewers of Paris.

A doctor and inventor, Marat found that his true calling was writing—and his true passion was the Revolution. He was a fanatic; some would label him a madman. He was physically tiny—almost a dwarf—with long, greasy strings of hair that hung over his eyes. He never bathed, and stank so that even his supporters would not sit near him at meetings. He suffered from a painful skin disease, which some said he had contracted when living in the sewers of Paris.

But while his physical presence may have been revolting, his writing style was gripping. "He appealed to people's deepest-seated fears and prejudices," writes one historian, "because his solutions were always direct and bloody, they all had the appeal of simplicity, not to say simplemindedness."[131]

About the threats from the prisoners of Paris, Marat did not mince words. His answer to the problem? Kill the prisoners—every last one. "I believe in the cutting off of heads," Marat wrote. "In order to ensure public tranquility, 200,000 heads must be cut off. . . . It is wiser and safer to storm the Abaye [one of Paris's largest prisons], drag the traitors out and massacre them. To give them a trial," Marat concluded, "is folly."[132]

Marat was unsuccessful in gaining a seat on the temporary council of which Danton was a member, but he was appointed to a different post—head of the new Committee of Vigilance. That committee was officially empowered to control the prisons and the police force of the city, but in reality was created to "ferret out all the traitors in Paris."[133]

Indeed, the Committee of Vigilance did not sugarcoat its function in its public statements. Official notices from the committee were put up all around Paris proclaiming: "The people must themselves execute justice. Before we hasten to the frontier, let us put bad citizens to death."[134] Under Marat's leadership, the Committee of Vigilance acted on its proclamations. Within a few days, it had begun massive manhunts throughout the city and the countryside, arresting those whom they accused of treason against the Revolution. Most of these were priests who still refused to take the oath of loyalty, and Swiss guards and aristocrats who had escaped the attack on the Tuileries.

"I Have Been Cutting Off Limbs Right and Left"

Such actions set the stage for a gruesome chapter of the French Revolution that has been called "the September Massacres." Early in September gangs of citizens began brutally killing the inmates of the Paris prisons.

The first victims were priests, traveling by coach to one of the city's prisons. A mob armed with sabers, clubs, and knives attacked the coach and dragged the priests into the street, where they were hacked to pieces. The National Guard, who were supposedly guarding the prisoners, stood idly by as the mob continued its grisly work.

Mobs moved from prison to prison, sometimes setting up tables for an impromptu court. A "judge" would ask questions of the prisoners, and, no matter what the answers, would sentence them to death. It was not only that these prisoners were being killed that was so appalling, say historians; it was the way in which they were put to death. "One man would knock the condemned man unconscious," says one expert. "A second would

A man reads off the names of imprisoned aristocrats that have been sentenced to death. Unruly mobs butchered between 1100 and 1500 prisoners.

cut off his head; then a third would skewer the head to the end of his pike and hold it aloft for all to see."[135]

After an hour or two of such work, passersby would notice blood running from the prisons into the streets beyond. One witness heard one of the executioners, covered from head to toe with blood, complaining, "For the last two hours I have been cutting off limbs right and left and I am wearier than a mason who has been slapping plaster for two days."[136]

The slaughter went on for days. When the executioners tired, they took naps just a few feet from the accumulating heaps of bodies—most missing heads or limbs. "It was about two o'clock when the butchers, tired out and no longer able to lift their arms . . . were sitting in a ring round the corpses lying opposite the prison to take a breath," remembered one witness.[137]

When they were working, their savagery was terrifying. Witnesses wrote later of the animal-like howling of the mobs as they began butchering their victims. Many of the corpses were sexually abused by the mob, and some body parts were eaten. One man recalled that during the butchering a woman came by with a basket of rolls for the executioners. "They took them from her," he says, "and soaked each piece in the blood of their palpitating victims. No cannibals ever behaved more ferociously."[138]

One of the most famous victims of the September Massacres was the young princess de Lamballe. A friend of Marie Antoinette, she was one of many aristocrats who were arrested after the storming of the Tuileries in August. At her "trial" she was told to swear to the Revolution, and to curse the king as an enemy of the people. Although she agreed to the first order, she told the man who was acting as judge that she could not betray Louis by calling him an enemy of France. Historian Clifford Alderman writes:

> Two men seized her. The street outside the prison was already strewn with bloody corpses. At the sight of the Princess, the mob howled with bestial ferocity. They did not kill her at once, but committed unspeakable tortures and indignities upon the wretched friend of the Queen. And at last they beheaded her.[139]

Historians say that the mob wanted to shock Marie Antoinette, and intended to

Princess Lamballe is tried and asked to denounce Louis XVI. When she refused, she was brutally murdered and beheaded by the mob. Crowds brought her head on a pike to Marie Antoinette, who was a good friend of the princess.

show the head of the princess to the queen. First, however, they took the head to a tavern and drank round after round, toasting the "health" of the princess. Someone then had the idea that before greeting the queen, they should take the head to a hairdresser to curl and wash the bloodstained hair.

When this was done, the mob hurried to the Temple, where they gathered outside the queen's window. As the crowd cheered, the queen went to her window to see what the noise was about—and saw the head of her friend impaled upon a stick. Historians say that the queen fainted.

Reactions to the Massacres

During the five days of the massacres, between eleven hundred and fifteen hundred people were killed. Most of the victims were not counterrevolutionaries. Many were priests who had no intention of working against the Revolution, but who simply could not in good conscience take the oath of loyalty. Many other victims were even more innocent: women and children who had no idea why they were being called criminals. They simply had the bad fortune to have been imprisoned after the storming of the Tuileries—people who had done no more than work for the king and queen.

The reaction of many around the world who were following the events in France was one of horror. The *Times* (London) asked scornfully, "Are these the 'Rights of Man'? Is this the Liberty of Human Nature? The most savage four footed tyrants that range the unexplored deserts of Africa, in point of tenderness, rise superior to these two-legged Parisian animals." [140]

Many in France agreed, and were both ashamed and repulsed by the savagery in their country. One witness who had been very supportive about the reforms of the Revolution wrote to her friend:

> You know my enthusiasm for the Revolution; well, I am ashamed of it! Its reputation is tarnished by these scoundrels, it is becoming hideous! In a week from now . . . who knows what will have happened? It is degrading to stay here, but it is forbidden to leave Paris; we are being shut in so that we can have our throats cut at their convenience. Adieu: if it is too late for us, save the rest of France from the crimes of these madmen. [141]

Most were convinced that not all Frenchmen, nor even all revolutionaries, were behind the September Massacres. Most of the butchers were the radical element of Paris, the sansculottes. Their ranks were increased by criminals who frankly enjoyed killing, as well as by common prisoners who had been released by the revolutionaries to make room for political prisoners. These were the ones responsible; much of France's population who lived in the outer districts, away from Paris, abhorred the butchery.

It was also important to note that influential people behind the scenes shared responsibility for the killing. While Danton and his political friends did not personally take up knives or swords and butcher people, they had the clout to stop it. And as for Marat—his part in the massacres was hardly subtle, with his daily writings urging his countrymen to behead all who were loyal to the king.

The Girondins and the Mountain

The differences in opinion about the direction the Revolution should take were evident at the new National Convention. (Since there was no longer a king in power, the new constitution was to be drafted by a convention.) The deputies elected to this convention represented two influential political groups, the Girondins and the Jacobins. Both believed that France needed a republican form of government, as opposed to a monarchy. However, the similarities between the two groups stopped there.

The Jacobins had incorporated many members of the old Cordelier clubs, and tended to be radicals, even endorsing violence on occasion. They drew their strength from the militant city government of Paris, the Commune. Although the Jacobins themselves were lawyers from the more well-to-do classes, they supported the sansculottes and other poor people. They were the party of Danton, Marat, and a deputy from Paris named Maximilien Robespierre. Robespierre, with his "icy, bespectacled stare and passion for impeccably tailored suits," would be a very important figure in the coming months of the Revolution.[142]

The Girondins were far more moderate than the Jacobins. They were from the provinces, not the city, and tended to reflect the country people's conservative political outlook. They were educated and idealistic; and while they supported the reforms that helped end the ancien régime, they were very suspicious of the rowdy mobs of sansculottes who ran wild in the streets of Paris.

The two groups sat on opposite sides of their meeting hall. The Girondins sat on the right side of the hall. The Jacobins chose the higher chairs on the left side, and because of their loftier position, were known as "the Mountain." It was fortunate that the groups were physically separated, say historians, because verbal battles between the Girondins and the Mountain were fierce, often involving personal attacks on one another.

Georges Danton, for example, was criticized by many of the Girondins for trying to seize power for himself and set up a dictatorship—a charge he categorically denied. "If there is any man so vile as to want to rule despotically over the representatives of the people," Danton declared, "his head will fall the moment he is unmasked."[143]

As the weeks went by in the autumn of 1792, it appeared that the business of writing a new constitution for France was hopelessly gridlocked, so uncooperative and hostile were the Girondins and the Mountain. Indeed, the convention often seemed more like a circus than an assembly. "The Jacobins repeatedly interrupted speakers with whom they disagreed," writes one expert. "Appeals were constantly being made to the spectators in the galleries. Legislation was slowed by demands for roll call votes, and debates regularly turned into name-calling contests."[144]

"Louis the Last"

One important issue that interested all people of France was the fate of Louis XVI. He had no active role in the government. Many laughingly referred to him as "Louis the Last" or "Louis Capet," that being the last name of one of his distant ancestors, an early king of France. To a man who was always addressed as "Your Majesty" or "King Louis," the rather ordinary "Louis Capet" must have been high insult indeed.

Since the storming of the Tuileries, members of the royal family had been held prisoner in the Temple, a six-hundred-year-old castle in the northeast suburbs of Paris. They lived in the castle's tower, with its tall, narrow windows and cold stone floors. They were mocked and laughed at by the men who guarded them, and when they were allowed out of the castle for a short time each afternoon, people yelled obscenities at the king and queen and threw stones and rotten fruit.

The imprisonment was only a temporary measure, as far as the Jacobins were concerned. They wanted the king executed as a traitor, or at least put on trial so he could be judged by his actions against the Revolution. The Girondins, on the other hand, tended to be less harsh. They hoped a trial could be avoided; as long as the king was locked out of the way, he was completely harmless.

The issue came to a head when in November 1792 a secret cupboard was discovered in the Tuileries. It held correspondence to and from the king that proved he was indeed trying to enlist the help of counterrevolutionaries to regain the throne. "Crammed with his secret papers [were] the plans for the flight to Varennes, and details concerning the money that the King had sent to the émigrés."[145] The evidence was impossible to ignore; the convention had to decide the fate of the former monarch.

"One Must Never Compromise with Tyrants"

Thus began a five-day deliberation in the convention. The Jacobins demanded an oral roll call vote, claiming that it was important for all to know which deputies would be traitors to the Revolution and vote in favor of Louis. The vote was unanimous—Louis Capet was guilty of traitorous activity against France. However, the stickiest question remained unanswered. What should be done with him?

The Girondins wanted leniency; after all, just months ago he was ruling France as God's

King Louis XVI before the National Convention. Although many at the convention wanted to spare Louis's life, they condemned him to death after finding incriminating papers in a secret cupboard.

After learning of his impending execution, the king's family members demand to see him to say goodbye.

representative. Even though the usual punishment for traitors was death, how could they execute a king? The Mountain was relentless. Death was the only answer, they declared. Marat even went so far as to demand his execution within twenty-four hours.

And so, on January 16 and 17, each deputy was given a chance to vote on the sentence of Louis Capet, traitor. One deputy, a Girondin named Vergniaud, said during his turn, "The law says death, but as I utter this terrible word I fear for the fate of my country, the dangers which threaten even freedom, and all the blood which may be shed."[146]

Georges Danton showed no sympathy. "One must never compromise with tyrants," he declared. "One can only strike at kings through the head; nothing can be expected from European kings except by force of arms. I vote for the death of the tyrant."[147]

It was, say historians, one of the most dramatic moments in history. Around the hall, each deputy was asked what his verdict

was, and each spoke his mind. When tallied, 361 votes—the majority—had been cast for execution. The king would die.

The Death of a King

January 21, the day after the verdict was announced, was selected as the day Louis XVI would die. In the morning, he was taken by carriage from his prison to the square where the guillotine was set up. The ride took just over an hour and a half. Along the route, a drummer beat a slow, steady beat. More than eighty thousand armed men stood shoulder to shoulder all along the route, a measure taken to ensure that there be no last-minute attempt by the king's friends to save him.

At the square, twenty thousand people waited to witness the event, many having sat in a chilly rain since dawn. Within a few moments of the carriage's arrival, the spectators saw what they had waited to see. Louis emerged, quiet and dignified, and mounted the platform where the executioner stood.

The executioner, a man named Sanson, tied Louis's hands with a handkerchief, and with scissors slashed off the king's ponytail and stuffed it in his own pocket. Before taking his place on the guillotine's wooden plank, the king looked out at the crowd and made a signal for the drummers to stop their beating.

"Frenchmen," he said, "I die innocent. I pardon the authors of my death, I pray God that the blood that is about to be spilt will never fall on the head of France. And you, unhappy people . . ."[148]

At this point, the executioner, who witnesses say seemed to feel Louis had talked long enough, signaled for the drummers to resume their cadence. The beating drums drowned out Louis's next sentences, and he was swiftly positioned on the plank. Within

A guard holds the king's severed head for the crowd to see. Moments later, thousands of citizens yelled triumphantly, "Vive la Republique."

a few seconds, the heavy blade fell, and his head dropped into the basket. Sanson scooped it up and held it for all to see. Historians say that the crowd chanted "Vive la Nation! Vive la Republique!"

There was a ghoulish aftermath to the execution. The crowds who had watched Louis die rushed to the platform to dip handkerchiefs and pieces of paper in the blood that drenched the area next to the guillotine. Others cut up the king's coat and vest into small pieces to sell. Even Sanson found a way to make money—by selling off pieces of Louis's hair.

Such activities offended some people in the crowd. One witness recalled seeing a man dancing around, laughing and singing, with his hands covered in Louis's blood. Another man chided him, saying, "My friends, what are we doing? All that is passing here will be reported. Men will depict us in foreign countries as a savage people thirsty for blood."[149]

Meanwhile, Marie Antoinette, sitting anxiously at the Temple, could tell the exact moment of her husband's death by the shouts and cheers carried for miles on the wind. Before long she too would fall victim to the guillotine's blade.

CHAPTER 9

The Terror

After the execution of Louis XVI, it became more and more difficult for the Girondins to keep control of the government. Up to this time, they were the majority in the convention, with the Mountain trying hard to undermine their power. That balance was soon to change, however, for the king's execution seemed to set a whole series of disasters in motion—disasters that would spell not only the Girondins' fall from power, but their deaths as well.

Enemies from Without, Enemies from Within

The news of the death of Louis at the guillotine alarmed the kings and emperors of Europe. They had watched nervously as the French people had restructured their government, written a constitution, and passed reforms aimed at bringing equality to their country. They had shuddered as the National Convention had declared that France "would bring fraternity and aid to all peoples that wish to recover their liberty."[150]

Those words had been worrisome enough. But now the people of France had beheaded their king! "If one crowned head could so easily be removed from its shoulders," writes one historian, "the others could hardly rest easy."[151] It was no great surprise when the forces of England, Holland, and Spain mobilized against France, less than a month after Louis's death.

For the Girondins, this new development was not a good sign. Although the French army had been victorious in a few lucky battles against the Prussians and the Austrians, they were ill equipped and badly trained. Adding three new enemies with powerful armies to the war could only mean disaster for the French.

Besides, France was far from united in its feelings toward anything. While the sansculottes of Paris had cheered the execution of "Louis Capet," the more conservative French of the provinces had been disgusted by it. Too, the repeated efforts of the government to punish the priests who refused to take the oath angered the deeply religious people of the provinces.

So angry were the provincial French, in fact, that when the government announced that three hundred thousand young men from the provinces would be drafted to fight in the war, there was open rebellion. How dare these Girondins and their radical government force their young men to fight in a war to spread the Revolution and anti-Catholic sentiments to other countries!

To make matters more complicated, there had been another season of poor harvests. Food was scarce, and because so much of it was being sent to the soldiers, it was even scarcer for the people in cities and towns. One historian reports that in Paris "the shortage of food became so severe that some people suggested that dogs and cats be killed for their meat. They were told that, if this were done, the rats in the city would spread even faster."[152] With no relief in sight, people rioted, destroyed and looted shops looking for money or food, and attacked food deliveries from the countryside.

The Jacobins Take Control

By early spring of 1793 the situation looked bleak for the Girondins. Foreign armies were poised on France's borders, ready to invade at any moment. Peasants were revolting in the countryside. Food supplies were almost at famine level. And the national treasury was almost empty.

The Jacobins, who had been the minority in the National Convention, relished the Girondins' predicament. Although Danton did try to get the two sides to work together, other leaders of the Mountain—Marat and Robespierre—called the Girondins traitors and scoundrels. According to Marat, every problem plaguing the people of France, right down to the bad harvests, was the fault of the moderates. For that, said he, the Girondins should be arrested.

"Your greatest enemies lurk among yourselves," he declared to the people of Paris. "They direct your operations, they direct your means of defense. The counterrevolu-

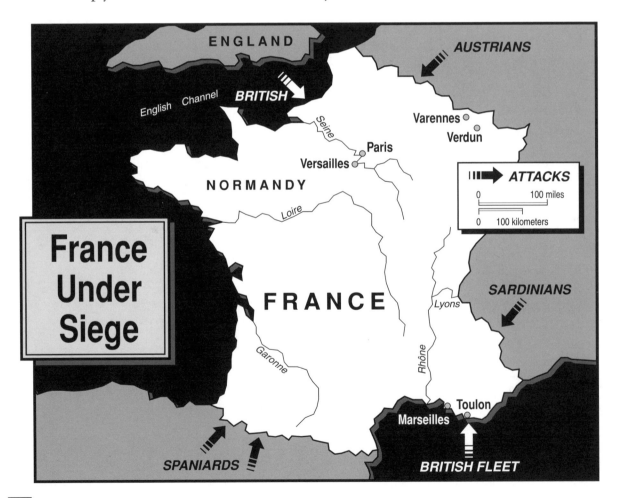

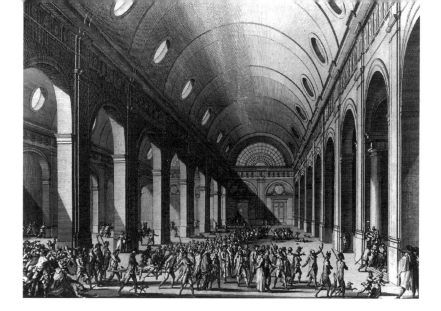

Thousands of armed Parisians demand the arrest of the members of the Girondin party who they suspected of having betrayed the Revolution.

tion lies within the National Convention. Among the deputies there are traitors and royalists. If you liberate them, our liberty is gone. If they are expelled promptly and for good, then the country is saved."[153]

Such well-chosen words were a deliberate means of stirring up the people. "Traitor" was one of the terms most feared by the common people, for it appealed to their fears that they would be killed by revenge-crazed aristocrats. Although, as historians say, there were hardly any members of the aristocracy left in Paris, Marat and Robespierre "kept insisting they were all over Paris, hidden away in the houses of the counterrevolutionaries and holding secret meetings where they concocted fresh plots against all true revolutionaries."[154]

By June 1793 the mobs in Paris were in such a frenzy they demanded the arrest of the Girondin deputies who they felt were working against the Revolution. In a massive demonstration on June 2, thousands of armed Parisians, together with thousands more soldiers of the National Guard, surrounded the hall where the convention was assembled.

The deputies were told that they would not be permitted to leave until the Girondin deputies had been turned over to the people. That day twenty-two of the Girondin leaders in the convention were arrested; no longer were the Girondins the most powerful force in the assembly.

Although some, like Danton, would have preferred that the unification of France's government happen voluntarily, other leaders of the Jacobins were jubilant. They had come into power, and the Revolution was in their hands. The fact that it had come about by bloodshed and violence was regrettable, they decided, but necessary.

Murdering Marat

After the arrest of the Girondin leaders, there was one twenty-four-year-old woman from the north of France whose anger could not be soothed. She had been a staunch supporter of the Revolution, at least until the Jacobins and the sansculottes had taken over. Her name was Charlotte Corday, and she had

had great hopes for the Girondins. They represented reform and change, yet with moderation. But now they had fallen, just as Louis XVI had fallen, to the violent mobs of Paris.

Corday decided to do something about the direction the Revolution was going. She decided to go to Paris and kill Marat, who she felt was largely to blame for the violence. In her mind, writes one expert,

> it was Marat who kept spewing out his messages of hate and urging the people on to further brutalities. Marat was the enemy of all the things she believed in, more vicious and bloodthirsty by far than

A fervent supporter of the Girondins, Charlotte Corday was determined to strike a blow against the sansculottes. She believed that murdering Marat would save the lives of innocent people whom he accused of being traitors.

the aristocrats had ever been in their days of power. Marat became the symbol of all of the hatred that had poisoned the Revolution.[155]

Her plan was to kill him in a dramatic fashion, preferably as he spoke at the convention. However, when she arrived in Paris, she learned that Marat was all but confined to his house because of his serious skin condition. Several times a day he sat in a bathtub, soaking in mineral salts to relieve the pain. It was there that she would kill him, she decided.

It was all very easy. She bought a long butcher knife, which she concealed in the folds of her dress. She also attached her birth certificate to a ribbon around her neck, so there would be no confusion about her identity when she was caught. (She had no intention of trying to get away afterwards.)

Admitted to Marat's bath, Corday found him soaking in the tub, a sheet wrapped around him except for his shoulders and arms. She plunged her knife into his chest, and in a minute or two, he was dead. Corday was caught and arrested; she denied nothing during questioning, saying, "I killed one man in order to save one hundred thousand. . . . I did not feel I was going to kill a man, but a wild beast who was devouring Frenchmen."[156]

An Instant Martyr

If Corday thought she was going to derail the Revolution by killing one of its leaders, she was wrong. If anything, Marat became more important in death than he had been in life. Never in all of French history did one man receive such honors after death.

His funeral was astonishing. His tomb cost an equivalent of $10,000—unheard-of in those days. His heart was removed from his body and placed in a vase of rare polished agate. The famous painter Jacques Louis David, who had immortalized various scenes of the Revolution, painted a death scene—a bloody Marat in his bathtub.

More than thirty towns and cities petitioned the convention for permission to change their names to Marat. Many babies born that year were given the name Marat as a first or middle name. His portrait was put on rings, bracelets, and necklaces. All over France, his picture hung in schools, and children were taught to make the sign of the cross when they said his name aloud.

The Rise of "the Incorruptible"

Maximilien Robespierre and Marat had been the most radical voices of the Revolution (Georges Danton had lost points with some of the sansculottes because of his call for compromise between the Girondins and Jacobins.) Robespierre was, say historians, as prim and proper as Marat had been scruffy and greasy, and as quiet and controlled as Danton was boisterous.

Although the elegant fashions and hairstyles of France had passed away with the ancien régime, Robespierre continued to dress like a dandy. He loved tailored suits, especially those of green and a silvery lavender, colorful vests, and an immaculately powdered, curled wig. His colorful dress was a sharp contrast to his personality, which historians say was humorless and austere. "He had a horror of laughter," one of his peers recalled.[157]

Robespierre led a very spartan life, favoring coffee and fruit for most of his meals. He did not like idle chitchat, but preferred long, intense discussions on issues of philosophy

Corday murdered Marat with a knife while he soaked in a bath to ease the pain of his skin disease. This idealized portrait by the famed painter David depicts the moment after the knifing.

and politics, which were his passion. He was an honest man, known to his enemies as well as his admirers as "the Incorruptible."

Robespierre was unyielding and rigid, as his politics demonstrated throughout the Revolution. Such rigidity kept him from truly identifying with the people he claimed to represent. "He believed in ideas rather than in men," writes one historian.

He had never been forced to work with his hands or to face poverty or starvation, and he was out of touch with those who had. . . . He demanded [from people] a dedication to the principles of the Revolution, and he was dismayed to find that they were more interested in food and better wages.[158]

Terror in the Countryside

The murder of Marat had enraged the people of Paris. More and more radical and violent, the sansculottes called for the government to do something about the dissension and counterrevolutionary activity. They demanded that enemies of the Revolution be rooted out and destroyed. The Committee of Public Safety—known simply as "the Committee"—seemed a perfect vehicle for this activity.

Soldiers and sansculottes band together to put down uprisings against the government. Under the leadership of Robespierre, armies were dispatched to put down revolts and kill the revolutionaries.

Robespierre had a major role in the workings of the Committee of Public Safety, a twelve-man council set up by Danton. The original purpose of the Committee was to carry out the everyday work of running France, to make sure that the laws of the convention were implemented. However, Robespierre and his cohorts transformed the Committee into a frighteningly efficient machine of terror.

The first order of Committee business was to deal with the revolts going on in the provinces. Many of these revolts were being led by men who still wanted a king for France. Some of these leaders were émigrés; others were supporters of the Girondins. The Committee dispatched armies to these wayward provinces, unleashing a fury of violence.

Peasants and their leaders were arrested, tried, and executed on the spot. Portable guillotines were hauled to the countryside to handle the executions. However, it did not take long for government officials to realize that the "national razor" was too slow—there were simply too many people who had to die.

Hundreds of people were lined up and shot, or blasted with cannon fire. At Nantes, two thousand peasants were forced on barges, which were towed out on the Loire River and sunk. And it was not enough that people died; horses, cattle, and hundreds of farm animals were slaughtered, too.

In places where whole villages or towns had revolted against the government, the Committee ordered the buildings destroyed by cannons, and whatever structures remained to be dismantled stone by stone. The town of Lyons was particularly odious to the Committee: After every structure in it was destroyed, "the name of the city was replaced on the maps with the grim word *sansnom*, 'city of no name.'"[159]

"Go Towards That House, Towards That Big Tree"

In Voices of the French Revolution, *edited by Richard Cobb, a state official of France describes both how much support the peasant armies had during the uprisings in the provinces, and how difficult it was to defend against their use of guerrilla warfare. This particular uprising occurred in Vendee in the early summer of 1793.*

"The rebel army never stayed together for more than three or four days. Once the battle was won or lost, nothing would keep the peasants together and they went off back home. Only the leaders remained, together with a few hundred deserters or foreigners who had no families to return to; but as soon as another venture was planned the army quickly took shape again.

Messages were sent all round the parishes, the tocsin was rung; all the peasants flocked in. Each soldier brought his own bread, and in addition the generals took care to have a supply baked. Meat was distributed to the troops. Corn and cattle necessary for supplies were requisitioned by the generals, and care was taken to have this expense borned by the nobles, great landowners and *emigres'* estates; but it was not always necessary to make requisitions; people were anxious to contribute voluntarily; villages subscribed to the cost of sending wagons of bread to meet the army as it passed; peasant women knelt saying the rosary along the route, offering supplies to the soldiers.

No one ever said to the soldiers, 'Right turn, left turn.' They were told, 'Go towards that house, towards that big tree,' and then the attack began. The peasants hardly ever failed to say their prayers before launching an attack, and they almost all crossed themselves each time they were about to fire."

"Let Terror Be the Order of the Day"

The Committee's work was not limited to the provinces, however. In Paris, Robespierre and his associates were assisted by the Revolutionary Tribunal. This was a court whose purpose was to sentence and punish those who were enemies of the Revolution. More powerful than other courts, the tribunal's decisions could not be appealed, and the sentences handed down were carried out immediately.

All of the members of the tribunal—judges, prosecutors, and even the jury—were appointed by the convention. According to its charter, it had the authority to try "all counterrevolutionary acts, all attacks upon the Republic and the security of the state, and all plots hostile to the liberty, equality, and sovereign rights of the people." [160] The definition of "counterrevolutionary acts," however, was greatly expanded by Jacobin lawmakers intent on wiping out dissension in France.

Priests not taking the oath of loyalty were to receive the death penalty automatically under the new laws. So were émigrés. Anyone wearing a white cockade (white being the symbol of royalty) was immediately arrested as a conspirator against the Revolution. It made no difference, under these new laws, whether the crime was committed by an adult or a child—however, girls under fourteen would not be killed, only exiled.

People could be put to death for speaking against any of the deputies, or against the convention as a whole. Anyone who wrote a pamphlet, an editorial, or even a letter that questioned the Revolution could be killed. Incredibly, husbands or wives showing regret when their spouses were killed for such offenses would receive the death penalty also.

To assist the government in identifying possible enemies, vigilance committees were set up all over France. One of their jobs was to hand out "Certificates of Good Citizenship" to worthy people. Those who did not receive a certificate—for whatever reason—could be arrested and imprisoned at any time.

And the reasons for not getting a certificate? The laws dealing with counterrevolu-tionaries were so vague that vigilance committees had a great deal of leeway in deciding who was a loyal citizen and who was not. For instance, one did not actually have to do *anything* to be considered an enemy of the Revolution—one law declared that one could be imprisoned who had not "constantly demonstrated his support of the Revolution."[161] Because of such vague laws, people were often imprisoned and executed who had done nothing at all.

This was the period of the Revolution known as "the Terror." In fact, the favorite slogan of the Revolution had become "Let terror be the order of the day." People spoke in whispers, if they spoke at all, for no one wanted to be viewed as a traitor. One man heard a neighbor tell his wife that Louis had been a decent man. The man reported the offense to the tribunal, and after a speedy trial, the husband was put to death. A woman was executed for writing a letter criticizing

During the Terror, anyone suspected of disloyalty toward the Jacobins was hauled off to the guillotine, including those people who remained loyal to the defeated Girondins.

An Afternoon at the Guillotine

As morbid as it may seem, the executions each afternoon were well attended by the French people, who treated the occasions more like a circus. As Clifford Lindsey Alderman writes in his book Liberty! Equality! Fraternity!: The Story of the French Revolution, *many people enjoyed the executions, and found nothing odd about treating them as an entertainment for the whole family.*

"When the carts [filled with prisoners scheduled for execution] turned into the Rue Nationale, once the Rue Royale, the doomed ones could see the Place de la Revolution, filled with a crowd whose red caps made it look like a field of poppies stirring in the wind. Many of the people had been waiting for hours in order to have a good spot, reading their newspapers, refreshing themselves with food and drink at stands put up there. Children frolicked, chasing each other like scampering squirrels. Peddlers wove in and out, crying, 'Little cakes! Nice little cakes!' It was like a circus day.

A lane had been cleared for the tumbrels. As they drew near, their occupants looked up in terror at the high platform with its glittering instrument of death. There stood the ruffian Sanson, whom some called the Butcher, though to his face they said he was the Avenger of the People. There stood his assistant, a true showman, with a rose clenched between his teeth.

The tumbrels moved up . . . halted . . . moved up. Their cargo, discharged, ascended the steps, some bravely, some assisted to keep them from collapsing. The triangular knife rose . . . fell . . . rose . . . fell with monotonous regularity, and in rhythm with a cadence of sound that rose and fell like the crash of breakers on a rocky shore."

---

the wife of a Jacobin deputy. One had to be very careful during the Terror; even though the Revolutionary Tribunal worked day and night, it could not keep up with the numbers of accused people brought before it.

Every afternoon the execution carts, called tumbrels, clattered along the streets toward the square where the guillotine stood. Its unlucky passengers were often well-known, as was the case with Marie Antoinette and captured Girondin deputies. At other times they were virtually unknown, those "denounced by malicious neighbors or personal enemies."[162]

And always, a spirit of festivity affected those who came to watch. Many brought picnic lunches and saved particularly good vantage spots for their friends and neighbors. It was as if Paris could not get enough of the metallic snapping of the blade as it severed head from body, or the cheers of the crowds as the bloody trophy was triumphantly displayed.

"Liberty, Equality, Fraternity!"

France was a dangerous place. It seemed to many that the Revolution had become a monster, gobbling up everyone and everything in its path. "No one was safe," wrote one witness to the Terror. "[The Terror] flew above all heads and chopped them off haphazardly, as arbitrarily and rapidly as the scythe of Death."[163]

Stepping Over the Line

The Terror was not confined to the masses, either. Those in power, those who enjoyed some favored status in government—those people worried, too. They lived in the fear that the finger would soon point to them, that their actions—or reactions—might make them look like enemies of the Revolution. One who lived through the Terror wrote that, to some in the government, particularly in the convention, "it seemed as if the only way to avoid prison or the scaffold was to send others there."[164]

The leaders of the commune, the city government of Paris, were eliminated for this reason. They had become too radical, too extreme even for Robespierre and the Committee of Public Safety. Led by Jacques Hebert, the Commune had called for the abolishment of Christianity in France. Hebert and his followers supported mobs of sansculottes who forcibly closed churches and forced priests and bishops to resign.

Publisher and member of the Commune, Hebert was guillotined after advocating the abolishment of Christianity in France.

Robespierre wasted no time denouncing Hebert and the Commune. He believed, correctly, that their anti-Christian views would alienate many supporters of the Revolution. He called Hebert a conspirator, and accused him of plotting the destruction of France. And because Robespierre was so powerful, and the Committee so feared, Hebert was through. He and his associates were arrested and guillotined.

"Show My Head to the People"

Robespierre's next political threat was Georges Danton. Always a popular figure, Danton had lost face with the most radical element of the Revolution by urging compromise between political factions and between France and its foreign enemies.

Danton spoke out against the Terror, too. He understood that Robespierre had high ideals and lofty goals for the Revolution. But, says one historian, he "scoffed at Robespierre's high-flown idea that the virtue of the people could only be achieved by wiping out the evil through blood. He knew the

As Danton approaches the scaffold he predicts that the people will turn against Robespierre and his followers in less than three months—a prediction that would prove to be deadly accurate.

French too well; he understood that they wanted food and security, not virtue and self-denial."[165]

Sensing that Danton was striking a responsive chord with the French people, Robespierre concluded that he had to be eliminated, too. Robespierre called for his arrest on trumped-up charges that Danton was a traitor and a threat to the people. It seemed farfetched at first to believe that Danton would be convicted, for there were many in government, including some of the twelve on the Committee, who liked and respected him.

But fear and the Terror won out, and Danton was condemned. His last words to the executioner were quintessential Danton: "Show my head to the people," he said. "It is well worth having a look at."[166]

The Fall of the Incorruptible

By July 1794 the Terror was having a pronounced psychological effect on the members of the convention. They were worn down, and highly dissatisfied with the direction of the Revolution. France had become a place of the dying, a nation with lofty ideals but with an unquenchable thirst for blood. As the public prosecutor of the Revolutionary Tribunal remarked happily, "Heads are falling like slates. Next week I'll take the tops off three or four hundred."[167]

Robespierre should not have been surprised when his colleagues in the convention formed a conspiracy against him, just as he himself had done to his colleagues. The last straw came on July 26, 1794, when Robespierre stepped to the rostrum at the convention and announced that he knew of enemies in the government—including some in the Committee. He had a list, he said, which he would soon share with them all. The solution, he declared, was to "purify" the Committee—which meant, of course, to execute some of its members.

One member of the Committee, Pierre Joseph Cambon, rushed to the rostrum. He and the other members of the Committee had had enough of Robespierre's "conspiracies" and enemy lists, he said. "Before I am dishonored," he cried, "I will speak to France. It is time that everyone here should know the truth. One man paralyzes the will of the National Convention. That man is Robespierre!"[168]

Others hastened to agree with Cambon, and a furious Robespierre realized he had lost the support of the government. Even so, he tried to appeal to the convention, but his attempts to speak were interrupted with shouts of "Down with the tyrant!" One fellow Committee member yelled, "The blood of Danton suffocates him!"

Following a futile suicide attempt in which he shot himself in the jaw, Robespierre was arrested. Lying in his cell, the man so famous for his dapper fashion, the cool, idealistic architect of the Terror, did not look so fearsome. "He did not stir," wrote one witness, "but he breathed heavily. He placed his right hand on his face; evidently wishing to conceal it. . . . He wore his sky-blue coat and his nankeen breeches . . . but his clothes were in disorder, and his shirt was bloody. He had no hat and no cravat, and his white stockings had slipped down to his heels."[169]

Finally, at 7:00 on the evening of July 28, Robespierre was loaded into a tumbrel and sent to the guillotine. As thousands cheered, his head dropped into the basket.

A Violent Legacy

The death of Robespierre was really the end of the Terror. The French people breathed a collective sigh of relief as the suspicion and anxiety were put to rest at the death of one

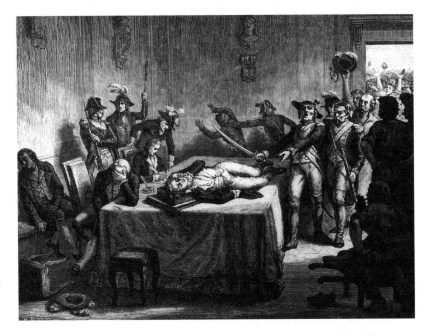

Robespierre lies wounded before the Revolutionary Tribunal, members of which believed him to have become increasingly paranoid and out of control.

What the Revolution Proved

The French Revolution affected more than just the people of France. All around the world, and for generations to come, the Revolution proved something, according to historian Sarel Eimerl, in his book Revolution! France 1789–1794.

"The French Revolution . . . was much more important than any of its leaders. More important than any of their quarrels. More important than the wars it had produced or its military victories and defeats. The effects of the Revolution have lasted till the present day. For the Revolution destroyed the old, unfair system in which a few rich aristocrats ruled France while the mass of the people lived in poverty. The Revolution proved that ordinary men and women could rise up against tyrannical rulers. It proved that every individual could enjoy the right to vote and be treated equally under the law. It enabled the peasants to own their own plots of land instead of having to work, like slaves, for the rich landowners. It gave the working men and women of the cities a new feeling of self-respect. It turned France into a democracy.

From France these principles spread out all over western Europe. Other people followed the lead of the French revolutionaries. They, too, rose up against the kings and the aristocrats who ruled over them and asserted their own right to share in the government. Few episodes in history have been as horrible as the French Revolution. But few have done more to improve the everyday lives of ordinary men and women. Many of the leading revolutionaries were butchers and liars, intriguers and cowards. As individuals, many, perhaps most, were despicable human beings. Yet through their actions and example, they helped hundreds and millions of people who came after them to win the right to elect their leaders, and so to live in freedom."

of the Revolution's most controversial leaders. A few more extremists were executed, but for the most part, the guillotines were finally idle by the end of the summer of 1794. It was then, too, that the end came for the Committee of Public Safety and the Revolutionary Tribunal, which had sent more than eighteen thousand people to their death during the Terror.

This was not the end of the Revolution, however. As Thomas Jefferson observed, "The generation which commences a revolution rarely completes it." That was certainly true of France. The dismantling of the grim political machinery of the Terror left the nation without a government. In the years to come, France would be led by a five-man council called the Directory, an emperor, three kings, and another emperor before becoming a republic in 1875—a process that played itself out for nearly a century.

In the months after Robespierre's death France witnessed a conservative reaction, a sort of backlash against the most radical reforms of the Revolution. However, it is important to understand that even at this time—even in the years to come when France was led by emperors or kings—the nation never returned to the strict conservatism of prerevolutionary days. There was, and would continue to be, a strong centralized government. There were no longer feudal rights; and the nation would be dominated by a strong middle class. The ancien régime was gone forever.

Experts differ in their assessments of the Revolution and its leaders. On the one hand, most historians say that it was a necessary and inevitable response to centuries of unfair laws and a repressive social structure. They point with admiration to brave men and women who were willing to take on that social structure and the politics of the day to try to change France. On the other hand, although the motivation behind the Revolution was idealistic and noble, the process was bloody and violent. As one expert writes,

"There was something horribly new and unimaginable in the prospect of a government systematically executing its opponents by the carload for months on end."[170]

The Paris square where the guillotine stood is still there. Its name has been changed from the Place de la Revolution (Revolution Square) to the Place de la Concorde (Harmony Square). The blood that ran over its cobblestones has long since faded, as have the happy crowds that once gathered to watch the Revolution's victims die. However, it is certainly true that the legacy of the French people and their leaders—Danton, Marat, Robespierre, and others—goes beyond violence. The motto of the Revolution lives on today anywhere in the world where people demand an end to oppression: "Liberty, Equality, and Fraternity!"

Notes

Introduction: What Could Have Happened?

1. Olivier Bernier, *Words of Fire, Deeds of Blood: The Mob, the Monarchy, and the French Revolution.* Boston: Little, Brown, 1989.
2. William Doyle, *The Oxford History of the French Revolution.* Oxford: Clarendon Press, 1989.
3. Bernier, *Words of Fire, Deeds of Blood.*
4. Bernier, *Words of Fire, Deeds of Blood.*

Chapter 1: Of Title and Privilege

5. Clifford Lindsey Alderman, *Liberty! Equality! Fraternity! The Story of the French Revolution.* New York: Julian Messner, 1965.
6. Georges Lefebvre, *The Coming of the French Revolution.* Translated by R.R. Palmer. Princeton, NJ: Princeton University Press, 1947.
7. Quoted in Emmet Kennedy, *A Cultural History of the French Revolution.* New Haven, CT: Yale University Press, 1989.
8. Lefebvre, *The Coming of the French Revolution.*
9. Doyle, *The Oxford History of the French Revolution.*
10. Susan Banfield, *The Rights of Man, the Reign of Terror: The Story of the French Revolution.* New York: J.B. Lippincott, 1989.
11. Banfield, *The Rights of Man, the Reign of Terror.*
12. Doyle, *The Oxford History of the French Revolution.*
13. Lefebvre, *The Coming of the French Revolution.*
14. Doyle, *The Oxford History of the French Revolution.*
15. Quoted in Doyle, *The Oxford History of the French Revolution.*
16. Doyle, *The Oxford History of the French Revolution.*
17. Doyle, *The Oxford History of the French Revolution.*
18. Doyle, *The Oxford History of the French Revolution.*

Chapter 2: The Downtrodden

19. J.F. Bosher, *The French Revolution.* New York: W.W. Norton, 1988.
20. Bosher, *The French Revolution.*
21. Bosher, *The French Revolution.*
22. Doyle, *The Oxford History of the French Revolution.*
23. Quoted in Doyle, *The Oxford History of the French Revolution.*
24. Quoted in Georges Lefebvre, *The Great Fear of 1789: Rural Panic in Revolutionary France.* Translated by Joan White. Princeton, NJ: Princeton University Press, 1973.
25. Quoted in N.S. Pratt, *The French Revolution.* New York: John Day, 1970.
26. Quoted in Pratt, *The French Revolution.*
27. Quoted in Lefebvre, *The Great Fear of 1789.*
28. Quoted in Doyle, *The Oxford History of the French Revolution.*
29. Doyle, *The Oxford History of the French Revolution.*
30. Quoted in Doyle, *The Oxford History of the French Revolution.*

31. Lefebvre, *The Great Fear of 1789*.
32. Doyle, *The Oxford History of the French Revolution*.
33. Quoted in Lefebvre, *The Great Fear of 1789*.
34. Quoted in Lefebvre, *The Great Fear of 1789*.

Chapter 3: The Seeds of Revolution

35. Bernier, *Words of Fire, Deeds of Blood*.
36. Banfield, *The Rights of Man, the Reign of Terror*.
37. Quoted in Bernier, *Words of Fire, Deeds of Blood*.
38. Horizon Magazine, eds., *The French Revolution*. New York: Harper and Row, 1965.
39. Quoted in Banfield, *The Rights of Man, the Reign of Terror*.
40. Quoted in Manuel Komroff and Odette Komroff, *Marie Antoinette*. New York: Julian Messner, 1967.
41. Komroff and Komroff, *Marie Antoinette*.
42. Horizon, *The French Revolution*.
43. Quoted in Doyle, *The Oxford History of the French Revolution*.
44. Komroff and Komroff, *Marie Antoinette*.
45. Quoted in Pratt, *The French Revolution*.
46. Banfield, *The Rights of Man, the Reign of Terror*.
47. Quoted in Richard Cobb, ed., *Voices of the French Revolution*. Topsfield, MA: Salem House, 1988.

Chapter 4: The Revolution Begins

48. Quoted in Cobb, *Voices of the French Revolution*.
49. Quoted in Cobb, *Voices of the French Revolution*.
50. Horizon, *The French Revolution*.
51. Quoted in Doyle, *The Oxford History of the French Revolution*.
52. Quoted in Doyle, *The Oxford History of the French Revolution*.
53. Quoted in Cobb, *Voices of the French Revolution*.
54. Banfield, *The Rights of Man, the Reign of Terror*.
55. Quoted in Douglas Liversidge, *The Day the Bastille Fell*. New York: Franklin Watts, 1972.
56. Quoted in Horizon, *The French Revolution*.
57. Quoted in Peter Burley, *Witness to the Revolution: American and British Commentators in France 1788–94*. London: Weidenfeld and Nicolson, 1989.
58. Quoted in Pratt, *The French Revolution*.
59. Doyle, *The Oxford History of the French Revolution*.
60. Doyle, *The Oxford History of the French Revolution*.
61. Quoted in Banfield, *The Rights of Man, the Reign of Terror*.
62. Bernier, *Words of Fire, Deeds of Blood*.
63. Quoted in Liversidge, *The Day the Bastille Fell*.
64. Quoted in Liversidge, *The Day the Bastille Fell*.
65. Bernier, *Words of Fire, Deeds of Blood*.
66. Quoted in Liversidge, *The Day the Bastille Fell*.
67. Horizon, *The French Revolution*.
68. Liversidge, *The Day the Bastille Fell*.
69. Liversidge, *The Day the Bastille Fell*.
70. Horizon, *The French Revolution*.

Chapter 5: The Citizens Take Charge

71. Quoted in Cobb, *Voices of the French Revolution.*
72. Banfield, *The Rights of Man, the Reign of Terror.*
73. Quoted in Doyle, *The Oxford History of the French Revolution.*
74. Quoted in Burley, *Witness to the Revolution.*
75. Sarel Eimerl, *Revolution! France 1789–1794.* New York: Little, Brown, 1967.
76. Quoted in Cobb, *Voices of the French Revolution.*
77. Alderman, *Liberty! Equality! Fraternity!*
78. Quoted in Cobb, *Voices of the French Revolution.*
79. Eimerl, *Revolution!*
80. Bernier, *Words of Fire, Deeds of Blood.*
81. Banfield, *The Rights of Man, the Reign of Terror.*
82. Quoted in Bernier, *Words of Fire, Deeds of Blood.*
83. Quoted in Bernier, *Words of Fire, Deeds of Blood.*
84. Quoted in Bernier, *Words of Fire, Deeds of Blood.*
85. Quoted in Cobb, *Voices of the French Revolution.*
86. Quoted in Eimerl, *Revolution!*
87. Quoted in Alderman, *Liberty! Equality! Fraternity!*

Chapter 6: "There Is No Longer a King in France"

88. Bernier, *Words of Fire, Deeds of Blood.*
89. Alderman, *Liberty! Equality! Fraternity!*
90. Banfield, *The Rights of Man, the Reign of Terror.*
91. Banfield, *The Rights of Man, the Reign of Terror.*
92. Eimerl, *Revolution!*
93. Quoted in Eimerl, *Revolution!*
94. Banfield, *The Rights of Man, the Reign of Terror.*
95. Horizon, *The French Revolution.*
96. Quoted in Bernier, *Words of Fire, Deeds of Blood.*
97. Quoted in Cobb, *Voices of the French Revolution.*
98. Quoted in Bernier, *Words of Fire, Deeds of Blood.*
99. Bernier, *Words of Fire, Deeds of Blood.*
100. Quoted in Banfield, *The Rights of Man, the Reign of Terror.*
101. Bernier, *Words of Fire, Deeds of Blood.*
102. Eimerl, *Revolution!*
103. Eimerl, *Revolution!*
104. Eimerl, *Revolution!*
105. Quoted in Bernier, *Words of Fire, Deeds of Blood.*
106. Quoted in Burley, *Witness to the Revolution.*

Chapter 7: France on the March

107. Bernier, *Words of Fire, Deeds of Blood.*
108. Quoted in Bernier, *Words of Fire, Deeds of Blood.*
109. Eimerl, *Revolution!*
110. Quoted in Pratt, *The French Revolution.*
111. Quoted in Cobb, *Voices of the French Revolution.*
112. Quoted in Banfield, *The Rights of Man, the Reign of Terror.*
113. Quoted in Cobb, *Voices of the French Revolution.*
114. Quoted in Eimerl, *Revolution!*
115. Horizon, *The French Revolution.*
116. Quoted in Komroff and Komroff, *Marie Antoinette.*
117. Quoted in Bernier, *Words of Fire, Deeds of Blood.*
118. Quoted in Bernier, *Words of Fire, Deeds of Blood.*

119. Quoted in Alderman, *Liberty! Equality! Fraternity!*
120. Quoted in Georges Pernoud and Sabine Flaissier, eds., *The French Revolution.* New York: G.P. Putnam's Sons, 1960.
121. Quoted in Komroff and Komroff, *Marie Antoinette.*
122. Quoted in Bernier, *Words of Fire, Deeds of Blood.*
123. Komroff and Komroff, *Marie Antoinette.*
124. Quoted in Bernier, *Words of Fire, Deeds of Blood.*
125. Horizon, *The French Revolution.*
126. Banfield, *The Rights of Man, the Reign of Terror.*

Chapter 8: Down with the King!

127. Horizon, *The French Revolution.*
128. John Haycraft, *In Search of the French Revolution: Journeys Through France.* London: Secker and Warburg, 1989.
129. Quoted in Bernier, *Words of Fire, Deeds of Blood.*
130. Quoted in Cobb, *Voices of the French Revolution.*
131. Bernier, *Words of Fire, Deeds of Blood.*
132. Quoted in Cobb, *Voices of the French Revolution.*
133. Quoted in Cobb, *Voices of the French Revolution.*
134. Quoted in Pernoud and Flaissier, *The French Revolution.*
135. Eimerl, *Revolution!*
136. Quoted in Pernoud and Flaissier, *The French Revolution.*
137. Quoted in Pernoud and Flaissier, *The French Revolution.*
138. Quoted in Elizabeth Wormeley Latimer, *My Scrap-Book of the French Revolution.* Chicago: A.C. McClurg, 1899.
139. Alderman, *Liberty! Equality! Fraternity!*
140. Quoted in Cobb, *Voices of the French Revolution.*
141. Quoted in Cobb, *Voices of the French Revolution.*
142. Banfield, *The Rights of Man, the Reign of Terror.*
143. Quoted in Banfield, *The Rights of Man, the Reign of Terror.*
144. Banfield, *The Rights of Man, the Reign of Terror.*
145. Horizon, *The French Revolution.*
146. Quoted in Cobb, *Voices of the French Revolution.*
147. Quoted in Cobb, *Voices of the French Revolution.*
148. Quoted in Eimerl, *Revolution!*
149. Quoted in Latimer, *My Scrap-Book of the French Revolution.*

Chapter 9: The Terror

150. Quoted in Banfield, *The Rights of Man, the Reign of Terror.*
151. Time-Life Books, eds., *Winds of Revolution: Time Frame AD 1700–1800.* Alexandria, VA: Time-Life Books, 1990.
152. Eimerl, *Revolution!*
153. Quoted in Eimerl, *Revolution!*
154. Eimerl, *Revolution!*
155. Eimerl, *Revolution!*
156. Quoted in Latimer, *My Scrap-Book of the French Revolution.*
157. Quoted in Banfield, *The Rights of Man, the Reign of Terror.*
158. Horizon, *The French Revolution.*
159. Horizon, *The French Revolution.*
160. Quoted in Latimer, *My Scrap-Book of the French Revolution.*
161. Quoted in Eimerl, *Revolution!*
162. Horizon, *The French Revolution.*

Conclusion: "Liberty, Equality, Fraternity!"

163. Quoted in Bernier, *Words of Fire, Deeds of Blood.*
164. Quoted in Bernier, *Words of Fire, Deeds of Blood.*
165. Horizon, *The French Revolution.*
166. Quoted in Cobb, *Voices of the French Revolution.*
167. Quoted in Eimerl, *Revolution!*
168. Quoted in Banfield, *The Rights of Man, the Reign of Terror.*
169. Quoted in Latimer, *My Scrap-Book of the French Revolution.*
170. Doyle, *The Oxford History of the French Revolution.*

For Further Reading

Daniel Arasse, *The Guillotine and the Terror.* Translated by Christopher Miller. London: Penguin Press, 1987. A well-researched history of the guillotine and its impact on the Revolution.

Steven G. Reinhardt and Elisabeth A. Cawthon, eds., *Essays on the French Revolution: Paris and the Provinces.* Arlington: Texas A&M University Press, 1992. Helpful essay on the relationship of the church and the Revolution.

George Rude, *The Crowd in the French Revolution.* Westport, CT: Greenwood Press, 1959. A good account of mob violence and the power of the Revolution's leaders. Excellent glossary.

———, *The French Revolution.* New York: Weidenfeld and Nicolson, 1988. Excellent series of maps of Paris, and good chapter on the power struggles between Girondins and Jacobins.

Albert Soboul, *A Short History of the French Revolution 1789–1799.* Berkeley: University of California Press, 1965. Difficult reading but helpful section on social structure of France.

Works Consulted

Clifford Lindsey Alderman, *Liberty! Equality! Fraternity! The Story of the French Revolution.* New York: Julian Messner, 1965. Easily understood account, told in story form.

Susan Banfield, *The Rights of Man, the Reign of Terror: The Story of the French Revolution.* New York: J.B. Lippincott, 1989. Highly readable account of the Revolution; excellent subsections on interesting characters of the time.

Olivier Bernier, *Words of Fire, Deeds of Blood: The Mob, the Monarchy, and the French Revolution.* Boston: Little, Brown, 1989. Extremely well documented; excellent index.

J.F. Bosher, *The French Revolution.* New York: W.W. Norton, 1988. Helpful notes for extended research.

Peter Burley, *Witness to the Revolution: American and British Commentators in France 1788–94.* London: Weidenfeld and Nicolson, 1989. A most interesting look at the Revolution and its leaders through the eyes of Jefferson, Morris, Young, and other visitors.

Richard Cobb, ed., *Voices of the French Revolution.* Topsfield, MA: Salem House, 1988. An invaluable reference; good primary source quotations, excellent illustrations.

William Doyle, *The Oxford History of the French Revolution.* Oxford: Clarendon Press, 1989. Difficult reading for a beginner, but invaluable notes and index.

Sarel Eimerl, *Revolution! France 1789–1794.* Boston: Little, Brown, 1967. Very readable account of the Revolution.

John Haycraft, *In Search of the French Revolution: Journeys Through France.* London: Secker and Warburg, 1989. Fascinating view of history seen through the eyes of a modern tourist in France.

Horizon Magazine, eds., *The French Revolution.* New York: Harper and Row, 1965. Well illustrated; good section on the Jacobins.

Emmet Kennedy, *A Cultural History of the French Revolution.* New Haven, CT: Yale University Press, 1989. Excellent notes and index.

Manuel Komroff and Odette Komroff, *Marie Antoinette.* New York: Julian Messner, 1967. Easy reading, but well-documented biography of the queen of France.

Elizabeth Wormeley Latimer, *My Scrap-Book of the French Revolution.* Chicago: A.C. McClurg, 1899. A valuable compilation of remembrances; great quotations, especially concerning the Terror.

Georges Lefebvre, *The Coming of the French Revolution.* Translated by R.R. Palmer. Princeton, NJ: Princeton University Press, 1947. Considered one of the most well-researched histories of the causes of the Revolution.

————, *The Great Fear of 1789: Rural Panic in Revolutionary France.* Translated by Joan White. Princeton, NJ: Princeton University Press, 1973. Helpful quotations from this early stage in the Revolution.

Douglas Liversidge, *The Day the Bastille Fell.* New York: Franklin Watts, 1972. Good source for young people; several good illustrations.

Georges Pernoud and Sabine Flaissier, eds., *The French Revolution.* New York: G.P. Putnam's Sons, 1960. Skillfully assembled compilation of good quotations from witnesses to the Revolution.

N.S. Pratt, *The French Revolution.* New York: John Day, 1970. Helpful source; good chronology in appendix.

Time-Life Books, eds., *Winds of Revolution: Time Frame AD 1700–1800.* Alexandria, VA: Time-Life Books, 1990. Well-illustrated, brief overview of time period.

Index

Picture Credits

About the Author

Gail B. Stewart received her undergraduate degree from Gustavus Adolphus College in St. Peter, Minnesota. She did her graduate work in English, linguistics, and curriculum study at the College of St. Thomas and the University of Minnesota. Stewart taught English and reading for more than ten years.

She has written over forty-eight books for young people, including a six-part series called *Living Spaces*. She has written several books for Lucent Books including *Drug Trafficking* and *Acid Rain*.

Stewart and her husband live in Minneapolis with their three sons, two dogs, and a cat. She enjoys reading (especially children's books) and playing tennis.